Human Rights Education

Issues and Challenges

Human Rights Education

Issues and Challenges

Edited by

Pratyush Vatsala

ATLANTIC

PUBLISHERS & DISTRIBUTORS (P) LTD

Published by
ATLANTIC
PUBLISHERS & DISTRIBUTORS (P) LTD
7/22, Ansari Road, Darya Ganj, New Delhi-110002
Phones : +91-11-40775252, 23273880, 23275880, 23280451
Fax : +91-11-23285873
Web : www.atlanticbooks.com
E-mail : orders@atlanticbooks.com

Branch Office
5, Nallathambi Street, Wallajah Road, Chennai-600002
Phones : +91-44-48531784, 28411383
E-mail : chennai@atlanticbooks.com

Reprint 2019

Printed in India at Nice Printing Press, A-33/3A, Site-IV,
Industrial Area, Sahibabad, Ghaziabad, U.P.

Preface

God has created man in His own image, says the Holy Bible. Our scriptures sing the glory of human birth, for which, even gods are covetous. How can such a human birth be abused by living a deprived life? Human birth gives us an opportunity to work and earn for both the worlds, be it earth or heaven. A life of dignity and respect is a human right and we need to be sensitive towards the dignity of each human being, irrespective of caste, creed, religion or sex. In other words, to appreciate human body, mind and spirit, to live the life in its true sense, we need to be educated in human rights. This book contains deliberations on the issues to sensitize us, to live to evolve a culture of human rights for a better future, wherein each one responds not to the 'other' but to his fellow beings with a sense of responsibility to society, country, environment and the world at large.

Humanity, as it has witnessed two world wars and stands shattered and battered by the developmental forces, expresses itself through the United Declaration of Human Rights (UDHR), containing thirty articles, ensuring life, freedom, security, movement, and above all, the dignity and respect of man. Human rights are, in fact, the "inalienable rights" of the human family and form the foundation of freedom, justice and peace in the world. Hoping to fulfil the highest aspirations of the common people for a society, free from fear and want, and to promote social progress and better standards of life, freedom of choice and a common understanding of all these rights and freedoms, the UN General Assembly proclaims,

> "Universal Declaration of Human Rights as a common standard of achievement for all peoples and all nations, to the end that every individual and every organ of society, keeping this Declaration constantly in mind, shall strive by teaching and education to promote respect for these rights and freedoms and by progressive measures, national and international, to secure their universal and effective recognition and observance, both among the peoples of Member States themselves and among the peoples of territories under their jurisdiction."

There are many instruments to ensure the implementation and realization of human rights but there needs to be a culture of human rights and of course, education is always a positive intervention in the process. Establishing a 'culture' for human rights is also important when it comes to be a citizen of a global village that the world has become and transboundary issues and challenges to development bring us closer each day. Human Rights Education (HRE) as an empowering tool to know one's own rights, the rights of others with a focus on the impetus to develop together, engages us with the commitment to discuss and adopt this culture which contributes to long-term prevention of human rights violations and value conflicts with peace building.

Vienna Declaration propelled UN Decade for Human Rights Education from 1995 to 2004 which emphasized the need of sensitising and teaching of human rights to the world, though, in 1953, with UNESCO Associated Schools Program, an "initial attempt to teach human rights in formal school settings" was formally initiated. The foundation for realizing this need was really set way back in 1974 with UNESCO's article "Recommendation", which expressed concerns for Education for International Understanding, Cooperation and Peace, and Education Relating to Human Rights and Fundamental Freedoms. Since then, UNESCO has a key role to play in promoting HRE through different development projects and programs at national and sub-regional levels. The responsibility of learning materials, its publication, translation and adaptation in national and local languages, advocacy and networking activities is also borne by the UNESCO.

Efforts are being made to define and design the curricula for this dynamic and broad concept of HRE. The International Congress on the Teaching of Humans Rights which met in 1978 agreed upon including the encouragement of tolerant attitudes with focus on respect. It also advocated the contextual knowledge of human rights with national and international dimensions and implementations, thereby developing awareness of human rights translating into reality. The World Conference on Human Rights in 1993 brought the issue of educating formally. It was two years later that the United Nations approved the Decade for Human Rights Education.

Following the decade of HRE, the General Assembly initiated the World Programme of Action which seeks to promote a common understanding of the basic principles and methodologies providing a concrete framework from international level to grass-roots level so as to advance HRE programmes in all sectors. Since then, the incorporation of HRE into formal school curricula has been introduced, developed and diversified. Non-governmental organizations, intergovernmental organizations, and individuals dedicated to spreading the topic through formal education are taking a lead role in the activity. The theory, practice and contemporary issues were the key concerns of HRE.

The twenty-first century has more expectations from HRE as it is seen as an empowering tool, strategy for development, an agent of change for women's issues, and a legal prospective for law enforcement. Different models have been worked out at different levels, which include values and awareness, accountability and transformation, encompassing sociological and psychological aspects of HRE, giving freedom of choice, freedom of action and freedom to bear the results of action.

Human Rights Education programme is a positive intervention to understand and address deep-rooted social and educational inequities through the lens of critical HRE as it aims at the policies and implementation that humanity ought to adopt to move closer to realizing the dream of structural peace in the world, where, our race will enjoy freedom from all kinds of discrimination, violence and oppression.

Education is value addition to the life of man which cannot be taken away by any war, famine or disaster. But the kind of education which promotes critical thinking, active citizenship and respect for diversity and pluralism beyond economic return is desirable. Education is an empowering tool that can be used either way. It may bring about conformity, or it becomes the practice of freedom by focusing on the right content, pedagogy and the structure with human rights principles, through which, human beings can discover how to participate in the transformation of the world, making it a better place to live. HRE imbued with values, conflict resolution training, and thereby developing a world view of the nature of reality, human nature, the purpose of existence and the principles governing appropriate human relationships can provide a panacea to this fragmented world of fractured identity.

Anything based on the idea of developing together and developing for peace and harmony would be welcome. A human being should be trained to be happy and to contribute to the society by applying noble ideas to life. The concept of GNH consisting of food, water, shelter, health, education, clothes, happiness and, love instead of GDP, clearly indicates that the new dawn has come. It is a fact that all the authoritarian leaders responsible for genocide were highly educated but they were never exposed to human rights principles of existing together in peace.

If we expect such high destinies from HRE, many issues come up curbing the choice of human freedom in a civil society. The issues and challenges to analyze the phases and trends of human rights movement for further research, civil society structure, biomedical research ethics, gender equity in human rights framework, children's educational rights, cultural diversity, inclusive education, terrorism, environmental issues, tribals, crime against women, role of media, silent revolution in human rights education and future threats have been taken up in this book. I hope that the book ignites a new spark in the direction of developing new perspectives in HRE for the world to make it a better place to live. The issues of HRE must be balanced with inculcation of human values and building a culture of sharing and understanding, otherwise the exercise of educating rights in a violent world to violent people may badly fail us.

I am thankful to all the contributors who came up with burning issues and challenges and ultimately, made the venture possible. It is not possible to take up all the issues and challenges in one book. For the convenience and focus, the number of chapters is limited to 15 only. I am sure it would be appreciated by the scholars, researchers and the readers who are interested in human rights and believe in UN manifesto to bring about peace and harmony to the world by education of human rights and values by full development of human personality and create a culture of human rights, peace and understanding.

Let us be together, as desired by the Vedic seers—as time past, time present and time future—all become one and synchronize in the cosmic schema of things:

"*Samano mantrah, samitih samani, samanam manah saha cittamesam samanam mantramabhi mantraye vah samanena vo havisa juhomi.*"

(Rigveda 10.191.3)

Pratyush Vatsala

Contents

Contributors

1. Prof. Munmun Jha, Dean, Department of Humanities and Social Sciences Indian Institute of Technology Kanpur.
2. Savita Sagar, Ph.D. Scholar, Jamia Millia Islamia, Central University, New Delhi.
3. Subhendu K. Acharya has worked among several tribal communities in Odisha and Gujarat. Presently, he is pursuing Ph.D in the Department of Anthropology, University of Delhi, Delhi.
4. Prof. Pradipta K. Das, Professor and Head, Department of Anthropology, Guru Ghasidas Cental University, Bilaspur, Chhatisgarh.
5. Prof. Gautam K. Kshatriya, Professor, Department of Anthropology, University of Delhi, Delhi.
6. Dr. Bulbul Dhar James, Former Hony Director at Sarojini Naidu Centre for Women's Studies, Jamia Millia Islamia, Cenral University, besides being Faculty at the Department of Political Science, Jamia Millia Islamia, New Delhi.
7. Dr. Harsha Merchant, Principal, Swayamsiddhi College of Education, SNDTWU, Mumbai.
8. Ms. Asmi Siddiqui, Selected for NCERT Doctoral Fellow, Research Scholar, Ph. D. (pursuing) Jamia Millia Islamia, Cenral University, New Delhi.
9. Dr. Usha Pathak, Assistant Professor, Teacher Education Department. D.A.V. (P.G) College, Dehradun.
10. Dr. Chetna Thapa, TGT, G.I.C. Maharjali, Tehri Garhwal, Department. of School Education, Uttarakhand
11. Dr. Rajalakshmi Datta is presently a faculty in the Department of Economics, DBS(PG) College, Dehradun. She is an ex-faculty

of School of Social Sciences, Doon University and Department of Economics, HNB Garhwal (Central) University.

12. Dr. Azra Abidi, Assistnat Professor Department of Sociology Jamia Millia Islamia, Central University New Delhi.
13. Dr. Rekha Trivedi, Associate Professor Dept of Political Science, D.A.V. (P.G.) College, Dehradun.
14. Raj Kumar is a Research Scholar (Human Rights and Duties Education), Department of Human Rights, School for Legal Studies, Babasaheb Bhimrao Ambedkar University, Lucknow.
15. Dr. Ram Kalap Tiwari, Associate Professor (Rtd.), Department of Psychology, K.S. Saket P.G. College, Ayodhaya, Faizabad.
16. Dr. S.R. Verma, Associate Professor & Head, Department of Physics, D.B.S. (P.G.) College, Dehradun.
17. Dr. Madhu D. Singh, Associate Professor and Head, Department of English, SGRR PG College, Dehradun.
18. Dr. Sweta Tomar has completed her Ph.D. From H.N.B. Garhwal Univ. Srinagar.

1

Human Rights Movement in India: Trends and Prospects for Research

Munmun Jha

Human rights organizations in India differ in their origins, histories, ideological orientation and strategies of intervention, but they share the same basic perspective, to gather information and influence implementation of human rights by the state or the government. They have successfully carved out a niche for themselves in the Indian polity. The human rights movement is nearly 70 years old, yet it continues to develop and mature.

This paper is divided into three parts. In the first part, I outline the phases of the human rights movement in the country, delineating its salient features. I suggest that its history can be divided into three phases. In the second part, I highlight some of the main tendencies and issues that confront the movement that deal with the structure, nature, and future of the movement. Issues discussed are sustainability of the movement, its expanding agenda, the spread of awareness, the question of legitimacy, the threat of careerism, the importance of grassroots organizations, the role of professional and scientific associations, the possibility of a national organization, the issue of international cooperation, and the relationship of the movement with the government. In the third part, I suggest some further work that can be undertaken from a rights perspective.

1. Phases of the Human Rights Movement

In sociological literature, there is some debate about what constitutes a social movement, or a new social movement.[1] It is not my task here to enter the debate; however, it must be pointed out that these terms are regularly used in scholarly literature to refer to collective human rights response. For example, the term "new social movement" is employed by Gail Omvedt in her study of the Indian dalits, women's, farmers' and environmental movements.[2] The existing data on rights organizations and their activities suggest that there is an established human rights movement in India, despite some disillusionment among a section of the activists, especially those who were once directly associated with it.[3] There is also near agreement among the majority of the activists and scholars that there is a movement today, even if there are questions about its spread, its functions, and its legitimacy.

Human rights with their modern attributes are a development more or less parallel with the growth of constitutional government and parliamentary institutions from the time of the British rule in India. The demand for civil and political rights was first raised by the Western-educated elite. It grew as a response to changes in the political system, and was incorporated in the nationalist ideology, championed by the Congress Party.

The first phase of the movement began with the formation of the Indian Civil Liberties Union (ICLU) in 1936, established by Jawaharlal Nehru. This phase came to an end in 1947, when the organization was formally disbanded. The importance of ICLU lies in the fact that it contributed to an understanding of what human rights meant: the right to oppose the government.[4] This understanding served its purpose well in the colonial period, but perhaps also imposed a bias on the kind of work that was undertaken by the organizations in the post-independence period. The 1950s and early 1960s were marked by the near absence of any significant organizations, except for a few regional ones modelled after ICLU. These were highly informal and limited in their scope. Their concern was to focus on repressive preventive detention laws and the arrest of political activists. Each of these organizations became defunct once political prisoners were released or elections announced.

The second phase started towards the end of the 1960s. Tarkunde gives three reasons why it took almost 20 years from 1947 for the seeds of human rights to revive and the almost virtual absence of any significant organization during this time.[5] (1) After the national independence, people assumed and expected that "there were possibilities of real progress." (2) There were still some leaders in the ruling Congress Party, who had participated in the nationalist movement. The people had respect and personal admiration for them. (3) The disillusionment of the people and the potential leaders of the movement was gradual. The faith in parliamentary democracy began to be shaken towards the end of the 1960s. Indira Gandhi's policies and dictatorial tendencies further contributed to the awakening of the movement. But the immediate cause in the rise of organizations was state repression on the Naxalite movement.

The organizations formed in this period in the early 1970s [especially the Association for the Protection of Democratic Rights (APDR) in Kolkata and the Andhra Pradesh Civil Liberties Committee (APCLC) in Hyderabad] still had a very limited agenda: that of highlighting police brutality and agitating for the release of political prisoners. However, they added a further dimension to the strategy of the movement. They did not just collect information and petition the government like the earlier organizations. They called for the involvement of the people in their "struggle" and were militant in their approach. Their impact in this phase was limited due to the fragmented nature of the movement, coupled with the indifference of the media and public opinion.

The Emergency (1975-77) was a watershed in Indian politics in many ways and had a great impact on the human rights scene. This led to the third phase, with the establishment of the People's Union for Civil Liberties and Democratic Rights (PUCLDR) in 1976. Founded by Jayaprakash Narayan, this was perhaps the most significant all-India organization in post-Independent India. In counter distinction to the earlier phase, a large number of prominent intellectuals and political leaders extended their active support. The media, too, after becoming a victim to the Emergency laws became sympathetic to the cause of human rights. The Emergency thus contributed in making the concern for, and discussion of, human rights a part of the mainstream public discourse.[6] Further consolidation of the third phase started in the early 1980s, after the return of Indira Gandhi to power. This is when most of the organizations redefined and expanded their agendas.

2. Tendencies and Issues

The movement today is characterized by certain definite characteristics; at the same time there are some issues that need its attention in order to be more effective. I will discuss some of them briefly.

Sustained Movement

There is an interesting parallel between the decline of ICLU and the decline of some organizations during the Janata period (1977-80). In both these situations, some leaders thought that since those sympathetic to rights issues had come to power (in the government), there was no need for independent organizations. The experiences of the Emergency had impelled some leaders to recognize that a sustained effort was necessary; others were convinced of this after the return of Indira Gandhi to power in 1980. So unlike the earlier phases, the movement is now continuous. It continues to work irrespective of which political party is in power. Autonomy from political parties is integral to its development and effectiveness, though it often has to rely on political leadership for bringing about the desired change.

Expansion of Agenda

There is a noticeable change in the agenda of the movement. Earlier, it focussed on political prisoners; now it focusses on a range of issues, which forms a comprehensive set of rights: not only civil or political rights, but also economic and social rights. It is thus different from the "new social movements" (the dalit, women's, peasants' and environmental movements), which are oriented to single causes.

New and fresh initiatives have been a major factor in this expansion. The movement has focussed on conflict over natural resources and the politics of development, social tensions created by an assertion of community identity and communal riots, and questions relating to the position of women within the family. It has thus widened the human rights framework. This framework is being used for ushering in social change, especially with regard to the condition of women in the family. But there are some areas which are rather tricky—for example, questions of reform within certain religious communities. In these cases, the political leadership is inclined to ignore any demands for fear of being accused of interfering in religious practices, especially if it relates to minority groups.[7] These are thus "questions that cannot easily be sorted out within the domain of the state-citizen discourse."[8]

The movement's aim is to serve all people; its intention is not to neglect any section of the population, yet since the victims are mainly from the lower classes and castes, it has tended to focus on the plight of groups which have been traditionally oppressed, and those other categories of vulnerable groups such as refugees and migrant workers. The notion that everyday issues of exploitation and oppression should be articulated using human rights concepts is fast gaining acceptance both among the activists and the people at large.

Some organizations are taking into consideration the social and economic condition of the lower classes and castes in formulating their policies. This has already changed the way some of the issues were being looked at. For example, the APCLC in Andhra Pradesh has requested the Naxalites not to harm anyone from the lower castes; additionally, they are now perceived as having a "right to struggle" against the upper castes. A caste-oriented outlook has a significant impact on the structure and functioning of the organizations, as indeed some changes have already taken place in the APCLC since this became an issue.

The movement recognizes that the state is the most important player in the human rights field, and its most significant adversary. It is clear that it is keen to emphasize or highlight those violations which are perpetrated by governmental agencies or in conjunction with state authorities. However, it has also identified that the state is not the only adversary, but represents also various kinds of power structures. Thus from just focussing on the state, it has started focussing on local power structures of dominance and oppression. Some organizations (especially those of the left ideological orientation) also focus on the policy initiatives of the multinationals and other global institutions such as the World Bank and the International Monetary Fund. They question existing models of development and politics, and focus on those who are victimized by these policies.

The Spread of Awareness

The most significant contribution of the movement lies in its role in the growth of consciousness and awareness about rights. This is also the belief of the activists. For example, according to Sumanta Banerjee, "Now it is at least on the agenda which was not the case before."[9] Sinha elaborates this view: "Earlier no one could imagine that human rights was an issue on which people could organize or mobilize public opinion and work together; now people understand when one talks of human rights.... The greatest contribution has been to bring it on the agenda."[10]

The movement has successfully highlighted a number of issues, even contributing a term to the discourse, that of "encounter killings." People are now aware of the kinds of abuse that take place, and more importantly, they are becoming increasingly aware that these cannot be committed with impunity; and that if abuse does take place, certain remedies would be available to them. As a result, people are willing to come to organizations with their complaints. There has certainly been a change in people's attitudes. Torture or death in police custody does not go unquestioned or unchallenged any longer.[11]

The impact is visible. Reports by organizations are usually covered by newspapers, and political leaders have begun to show an interest in human rights issues. There have been instances of government ministers threatening to resign if some of the laws relating to preventive detention were not altered.[12] There is, of course, the question of preventing or stopping violations. This is a long-term goal. In this area, too, it might be said that the movement has had at least a restraining effect.

Legitimacy

Any organization which has anything to do with welfare or human rights is generally assumed to have some kind of respectability and legitimacy attached to it. However, the area of legitimacy remains a contested field. This is especially true in the case of organizations that refuse to take public notice of violence by armed opposition groups. The effectiveness of organizations depends to a considerable extent on recognition that their information is accurate and that their action is impartial. There is a need to cultivate an image of impartiality among the administrators, political leaders and the people at large.

The organizations jealously guard their independence and credibility. Their policy of not accepting foreign funding makes it clear that they will not trade their credibility, or even take the risk of appearing to do so, for any amount of cash. This is in sharp contrast to many of the organizations in the West, where each project necessarily begins by first exploring the avenues for funding, and in many cases, actually securing it before starting work. With "professionalization" it might be the case that funding will assume importance, as indeed it has among the developmental NGOs in India.

Careerism

Even partial success has brought dangers to the movement. It is so far strictly a voluntary sector, in the sense that no one gets paid for any work. But as human rights become more fashionable, activists are apprehensive that this might soon start attracting those on an "ego trip" or those who want to further their careers. They fear that if this happens, the entire movement will be brought into disrepute. It is a fear shared by many activists that any effort to make the movement more professional would have a negative impact on its credibility. Thus, there is an effort to retain informal structures. One reason for the failure of Amnesty's Indian section was that it had passed into the hands of "human rights professionals." A pamphlet by the People's Union for Democratic Rights (PUDR) warns: "The hype of human rights and global networks has given rise to careerist trends which pose an emerging threat to the hard won credibility of the civil rights movement in our country."[13]

It is inevitable that in a modern free-market economy, organizations would be established to profit from the sale of information, even if it relates to human rights. But the organizations in India are genuinely concerned that this may erode their credibility, and of the entire movement.

Grassroots Organizations

I would suggest that as a result of the efforts of the organizations, there has been widespread growth in the awareness of rights issues. This has partly contributed to the rise of many grassroots organizations which use a human rights framework. These organizations are active in their local areas, and take up issues which are relevant to the local population. For example, an organization was formed in south Bihar in response to a government proposal to establish a National Firing Range Project in a tribal area. (The representatives of this organization claimed that the project is likely to displace about 200,000 people in about 245 villages.) Such organizations sometimes take action locally. In this case, the representatives had approached the PUCL in Delhi for help.[14] The movement needs to build up a network with grassroots organizations, strengthen them and in this process strengthen itself.

This is also true of the other specialized or new social movements. The rights organizations recognize other movements as distinct, and consider themselves as complementing their efforts. However, they also come together with other movements and form alliances in taking up certain specific issues. For instance, the Peoples' Rights Organization (PRO) was part of a Human Rights Campaign on Narmada and participated in joint programmers with environmental groups in protesting against the construction of Narmada Dam.

Professionals and Scientific Associations

Professionals such as lawyers and academics, occupy most of the leadership positions in the organizations. This is understandable for professionals in India were greatly involved in the freedom struggle, and subsequently have come to play an important role in the management of the democratic apparatus. They sometimes use organizational fronts and combine the promotion of human rights with their professional roles. The law professionals (practising lawyers, and other law-trained personnel such as judges, law academics and law journalists) endeavour to secure human rights within the parameters of the existing legal system. Nowadays, they also make use of the Public Interest Litigation system. However, as J.S. Gandhi has pointed out, out of more than 2,50,000 lawyers in the country, not more than "a total of 250 lawyers throughout the country...are involved in the protection of the fundamental rights of the people," excluding the routine cases where a question of fundamental rights might be involved.[15] Academics have contributed to the spreading of awareness through their educative efforts, but their impact is mostly confined to the literate or already educated groups. I would therefore suggest that though, the law and academic professionals are an integral part of the movement, there is further need for their involvement and continued contribution to the movement, which must take full advantage of their skills.

The medical profession is potentially very important. Doctors can be directly relevant in documenting and exposing cases of human rights abuse, especially of torture or death in police custody. Medical evidence can be used to counter spurious police assertions that detainees died due to illness or an accident. However, the situation is complicated. It is not unusual for doctors to participate in the cover up of criminal acts by the police. An Amnesty report remarks that some doctors "clearly are unable to withstand pressure from the police to provide post-mortems which assist an official conspiracy to conceal the truth."[16] According to Sinha, vice-president of PUCL, "Doctors are very unhelpful. They make the post-mortem reports to help the police."[17] PUDR has publicly condemned the "appalling negligence of the doctors...if not of blatant collusion at least of fatal callousness."[18] Even the courts have had cause to criticize the medical profession for "professional misconduct."[19]

Amnesty has found the practice of using medical evidence very powerful. But in India, the involvement of the medical profession with human rights has been minimal. The medical profession is barely represented in the movement. There was an Amnesty medical group in India in 1986, but there is no evidence that they carried out any investigations.[20] The first report by a medical team was an investigation into the effects of torture on Nagas in Manipur who had been tortured 22 months previously by the Assam Rifles, a paramilitary force. The study team examined 104 victims, and established that nearly all had experienced "third degree physical torture," that many still bore marks of physical torture and "out of 104 examined 101 were found to be mentally unwell." As the report makes it clear, "For the first time, a medical study of this nature has been carried out on a large number of torture victims."[21] The doctors who carried out this study were from Calcutta. It was difficult to get the co-operation of the local Naga doctors who were politically unorganized and frightened of the paramilitary force in the area. Thus, the movement needs to build up strong links with the medical profession, with lawyers and academics and other professional and scientific associations.

A National Federation

The next question I ask is: Can the purpose of human rights be served by a single organization, a national federation of organizations? There have been unsuccessful efforts in this direction. At least one federation does exist: the All India Federation of Organizations for Democratic Rights (AIFOFDR). However, there is no permanent national structure. Some activists argue that there is absolutely no need for such federations as there is already ample and effective coordination among different organizations.[22] It must be said that there are limits to effective cooperation for organizations which have diverse identities and ideologies. However, it is not difficult to conceive of a permanent form of cooperation: to coordinate certain specific programmes, or an information clearing-house and data centre to gather and disseminate information on cases of violations and the action taken in each of the cases. This is an issue that has not received enough attention in the recent years, but is one that merits attention.

International Cooperation

The movement has so far tended to be insular. By this, I mean that organizational efforts are directed towards remedying the human rights situation within national borders. They have not made a conscious effort to extend their activity to the international sphere. The situation is understandable, given that they have limited resources and are often too busy responding to cases which arise in the country. Considering that grants from foreign sources give immediate rise to suspicion, and independent funds constitute an invaluable credential in India, it is rather difficult for organizations to engage in any international action.

However, the organizations have established links with Amnesty International (and Asia Watch to some extent). A few individual leaders also have personal contacts with certain international organizations such as the International Commission of Jurists. In the recent past, there have been signs that activists are willing to travel abroad to attend international conferences, even if these trips are funded by foreign agencies. It is now increasingly being acknowledged by some participants that the experience gained during such conference is useful in understanding how international bodies function.

It might be suggested that lack of solidarity, or rather lack of proper contact and regular communication, with international organizations removes the Indian organizations from participating in relevant developments around the world, a process in which they have the potential to make a positive contribution. Further, a better understanding of the international initiatives would enable them to make use of some of the resources (especially in creating relevant public opinion) that might be available to them through various international bodies or agencies, including intergovernmental or non-governmental organizations.

The Movement and the Government

The government response to allegations of human rights abuse has undergone a change in the last few decades. Till the 1970s, allegations were simply ignored; in the 1980s, the policy was to deny any allegations of abuse, while not replying to any criticism directly. In the face of mounting international pressure in the post-Cold War era of the 1990s, the government's approach has become somewhat more open. It now accepts that abuses take place, but points out that it takes appropriate action in such cases; it also focusses on abuses by armed opposition groups within the country, emphasizing that the police and paramilitary forces have to operate in difficult circumstances; it has permitted international groups to visit India for investigative purposes; and has also constituted the National Human Rights Commission (NHRC). This certainly gives legitimacy to the debates and discussions on human rights.

In spite of some positive developments, the government's attitude towards Indian organizations has by and large shown little difference. Bowing to international pressure, it has permitted Amnesty and other international groups and teams to visit India, but there is hardly any indication that it has started taking the Indian organizations any more seriously than before. It has used many tactics to distract public attention from abuses. This is done in several ways: by dubbing reports by organizations as unreliable or one-sided; calling them terrorist organizations, or friends of terrorists, implying that they are "anti-nationals" and "pro-terrorist," or what is worse, launching a direct attack on the activists. The harassment of activists takes many forms: investigation of their activities, not permitting them to hold meetings or to publish material, arresting them on false charges, or even, as alleged by APCLC, elimination in Andhra Pradesh. A Human Rights Watch World Report for 1992 clubbed India with Colombia as "the most dangerous places to monitor human rights;" it also provides instances of rights monitors being killed by government agencies.[23] This not only creates fear among the activists, but also has the effect of blurring the distinction between terrorist groups and rights organizations in the minds of the people, reducing their effectiveness.

The organizations are naturally distrustful of the government. This was explicit in their attitude towards the formation of the NHRC. However, some leaders in their personal capacities do have a working relationship with some senior political leaders, and can approach them directly. The organizations today need to make an effort to work with the government. As Rubin has commented:

> Long-term strategies for the protection of human rights in India will require the power of the parliament and administration.... When legal institutions are weakened, the civil liberties movement must take on the contradictory task of trying to strengthen the state in order to discipline it.[24]

There is no doubt that the government, with its huge power and resources can be of immense use in strengthening human rights in the country. While the usual plea is to curb state power, or misuse of the prevailing laws, activists also campaign for the effective implementation of some rights already enshrined in the Indian constitution. An appropriate example is the focus on violation of women's rights within the family, first taken up from a human rights framework by the People's Union for Democratic Rights (PUDR). The movement must take on the role of suggesting effective solutions to issues through the methods of creative use of law and state power. The NHRC now seeks to facilitate such endeavour.

The government has shown to an extent that it is willing to implement human rights norms in the country. It is a signatory to many international declarations and treaties related to human rights. Yet there is more to be done. It can (1) ratify international instruments that it has not, such the Optional Protocol to the International Covenant on Civil and Political Rights; (2) be more open about international monitoring—that is, accept international control and on-site inspection by international, both intergovernmental and non-governmental agencies; (3) provide more avenues for domestic protection of human rights; (4) engage in the promotion of human rights education in schools and colleges, and in the training of military, police and law enforcement officials; and most importantly, (5) develop and enforce a policy of protecting and supporting organizations working for human rights in the country.

3. Further Research

The systematic study of human rights in India is still in its infancy. Thus, there is enormous scope for further research in all aspects of the subject. However, I will concentrate on some major areas of immediate relevance.

There is a vast amount of literature generated by the organizations in the form of pamphlets, booklets and reports, focusing on various incidents of abuse. These are primarily descriptive. I would suggest that there is further need to study the literature produced by each of the individual organizations. One way to do so would be a systematic study of the contents of the journals published by them. It might be added that this would require language skills as some of the journals are produced in regional languages such as Bengali and Telugu. Due to slightly improved record keeping by some organizations, it should soon be possible to undertake comparative studies of cases. Such studies would provide an insight into the changing nature of the organizations, and the continued extension of their activities.

I have argued that one of the major contributions of the movement has been to extend and enhance rights consciousness. An empirical research to gauge the rights consciousness among sections of the population such as students, professionals, etc., in different parts of the country would fill the gap in the existing body of knowledge. Another question is the relation between the spread of awareness and the apparent rise in the frequency of some specific categories of abuse such as custodial deaths.[25] Is this due to deterioration in the rights situation? Or is it merely that more cases get reported and documented as a result of more awareness among the people? Empirical studies could perhaps explain the apparent rise in the frequency of specific violations. I would also suggest that studies of specific categories of rights abuse may be undertaken with a view to contribute to the area of policy studies.

I have pointed out that the human rights movement sees its role as complementing the efforts of other social movements in the country; indicated their current relations with international organizations; and detailed their attitude towards the government. I have suggested more contact and co-operation with other. It might be useful to investigate the scope or possibility of establishing a framework for multilevel cooperation among different organizations or social movements in the country, in the South Asian region, or indeed at the global level.

An expanded research agenda is necessary for understanding the movement and the issues facing it. This is due to the emergence of new categories of rights and the transformation of existing ones. As far as researching aspects of policy or activities is concerned, it must be mentioned that organizations can make the task of research simpler, if they paid some attention to record keeping. Further, some organizations have "internal records" and do not permit their members to speak to researchers. This is a hindrance in any research. The general attitude of organizations towards research is rather lukewarm. This is primarily because of the low value attached to independent social research by the political leadership or the government. Thus, the findings of social research usually fail to make any impact. It is perhaps not surprising that in such a situation, the organizations are probably unaware of the potential benefits of research on either themselves or the cause they are fighting for.

Finally, let me end by quoting Arun Shourie, a founder member of PUCL. In a survey report on custodial deaths, he rhetorically asks:

> How would you want me to end this survey—with the plea that the formal provisions of law should be adhered to, with the plea to the police to be humane, with the plea to the public to keep their anger from subsiding with such unvarying certainty, with the plea that we build up strong civil rights organizations, with the plea that the press do its job better? Choose the one you think will bear fruit.[26]

The answer is that there is a need for cooperation and better coordination among different players. The eventual aim is to create a society where no more vigilance is required and where human rights organizations are redundant. But, until such a time comes, unceasing effort must continue, an effort in which they have indeed a vital role to play. It remains to be seen if they can face the challenges that lie ahead, which remain as demanding as ever.

REFERENCES AND NOTES

1. Joseph R. Gusfield, editor, *Protest, Reform and Revolt: A Reader in Social Movements,* New York: John Wiley and Sons, 1970, pp. 1-8; J.A. Banks, *The Sociology of Social Movements,* London and Basingstoke: The Macmillan Press, 1972.
2. See Gail Omvedt, *Reinventing Revolution: New Social Movements and the Socialist Tradition in India,* New York: M.E. Sharp, 1993, pp. xv-xvi and 299-319; see also Andre Gunder Frank and Marta Fuentes, "Nine Theses on Social Movements," in *Economic and Political Weekly,* 29 August 1987, pp. 1503-10.
3. For example, see Sadanand Menon, "The Marginalisation of Civil Liberties Movement," in *Rethinking Human Rights: Challenges for Theory and Action,* edited by Smitu Kothari and Harsh Sethi, New York: New Horizon Press and Delhi: Lokayan, 1989, p. 37.
4. "Nehru and Civil Liberties in India." In *International Journal of Human Rights,* 2003, Volume 7, Number 3, pp. 103-15.
5. Smitu Kothari, "An Interview with V.M. Tarkunde," in *Rethinking Human Rights, op. cit*., pp. 133-50.
6. "Sustaining Democracy and Human Rights from Indira Gandhi's Emergency to the Present." In *Encyclopedia of Human Rights,* edited by David P. Forsythe. New York: Oxford University Press, 2009, Vol. 3, pp. 5-16.
7. See for example the demands put forward by the reformists in the Bohra community, who are led by Ashgar Ali Engineer, a national vice-president of the PUCL. Central Board of Dawoodi Bohra Community (CBDBC), *The Reformist*

Bohras: Their Problems and Demands, Bombay: CBDBC, 1990; CBDBC, *The Issues in the Bohra Reform Movement,* Bombay: CBDBC, 1991; CBDBC, *The Problems of the Bohra Community,* Bombay: CBDBC, 1991.

8. Smitu Kothari, "The Human Rights Movement in India: A Critical Overview," in *Rethinking Human Rights, op. cit.*, p. 94.
9. Sumanta Banerjee, Interview with author. New Delhi, 12 March 1994. Tape recording.
10. Prabhakar Sinha, Interview with author. New Delhi, 7 February 1994. Tape recording.
11. *Ibid.*
12. Two cabinet ministers in the P.V. Narashima Rao Government threatened to resign if TADA, a legistation that activists have been campaiging against, was not allowed to lapse in May 1995.
13. Peoples Union for Democratic Rights (PUDR), *Remembering C.V. Subba Rao,* Delhi: PUDR, February 1994, p. 8.
14. "Proceedings of the PUCL National Council Meeting, 5-6 February 1994," in *PUCL Bulletin,* Vol. 14, No. 3, March 1994, p. 6.
15. J.S. Gandhi, "Human Rights Efforts of Professionals in Contemporary India: A Sociological Examination of Some Select Evidence." Paper presented at IPSA Human Rights Conference, The Hague, 1-3 June 1987, p. 24.
16. In November 1986, the Resident Doctors Association of the prestigious All India Institute of Medical Sciences in New Delhi accused the police of "interferring in the professional freedom of doctors of the AIIMS." For details, see AI, *India: Torture, Rape and Deaths in Custody,* London: AI, 1992, p. 73. AI Index: ASA 20/06/92.
17. Prabhakar Sinha, interview.
18. PUDR, "A Theft and Death Sentence: Murder in Patel Nagar Police Station." Delhi: PUDR, August 1991, p. 4.
19. In one particular case, Idris Mian, a prisoner, was beaten by the police in full view of a large number of people. According

to Justice Deb, who carried out an investigation, the local medical officer "did not do his duty properly. He did not give any life saving medicine to Idris and did not deliberately record the injuries inflicted on Idris to save Calcutta Police." Later when Idris was taken to the Calcutta Medical College Hospital, the doctor "created false evidence which is not only an offence but is against his professional conduct. And he did it at the instance of some of those who brought the dead boy of Idris to Medical College." See "C.M. Asks for Stern Action: Assembly Walk-Out Over Idris Mian's Death," *The Statesman,* Calcutta, 29 March 1984; Government of West Bengal, "Memorandum of Action Taken on the Report of Deb Commission of Inquiry Regarding the Death in Custody of Calcutta Police on 28.3.84 of Md. Idris, Main Suspect in the Murder Case of V.K. Mehta, Ex-Deputy Commissioner of Police, Port Division." No date, pp. 1-2. Mimeograph.

20. D.S. Mehra, "Human Rights and the Medical Profession" in *Delhi Groups Commemorate the Twenty-fifth Year of Work for Prisoners of Conscience, Abolition of Torture and the Death Penalty with an Exhibition of Posters,* Amnesty International, Indian Section, New Delhi: AI, 26 October 1986, pp. 13-14.

21. Drug Action Forum, *Post Torture State of Mental Health: Report of a Medical Study on the Delayed Effects of Torture on Nagas in Manipur,* Calcutta: Drug Action Forum, July 1990; for details of the case, see Amnesty International, *"Operation Bluebird": A Case Study of Torture and Extrajudicial Executions in Manipur,* London: AI, October 1990, AI Index: ASA 20/17/90; see also Co-ordinating Committee on Oinam Issue (COCOI), *The Third Report,* Imphal: COCOI, March 1990.

22. Yogesh Kamdar, Interview with author. Bombay, 4 March 1994. Tape recording.

23. Human Rights Watch, *Human Rights Watch World Report 1993: Events of 1992.* New York: Human Rights Watch, pp. xvii, 169-71. For a recent example of harassment of an activist, see Y.P. Chibbar, "Harassment of Kamdar," in *PUCL Bulletin,* Vol. 14, No. 1, January 1994, p. 9.

24. Barnett R. Rubin, "The Civil Liberties Movement in India: New Approaches to the State and Social Change," in *Asian Survey,* Vol. 27, No. 3, March 1987, pp. 391-92.

25. See PUDR, *In Pursuit of Lofe: A Report on the Aftermath of Custodial Deaths in Delhi,* Delhi: PUDR, October 1991.

26. Arun Shourie, "Lethal Custodians," in *Violation of Democratic Rights in India,* edited by A.R. Desai, Bombay: Popular Prakashan, 1986, p. 322.

2

Human Rights Education and Civil Society

Savita Sagar

> To deny people their human rights is to challenge their very humanity. *Nelson Mandela*

Human rights are like a life support system for mankind and in its absence, life is nothing. The word, human rights, came into existence when the man faced mass destruction in the Second World War. Existing International organisations soon realised that there should be certain common standard of rights for human being and should be given to all people for simply being human. Human beings are entitled for their basic rights and fundamental freedoms. Thus, the human rights concept came into practice after universal declaration of human rights. But, if we see historically and theoretically, human rights have always been a subject of discussion and all developments of human society begin with rights. Rights based approach focuses on rights based human development. Now, this term has become a buzzword for every discipline. Humanistic approach towards any development is being considered as an important factor. Here the question arises whether mere mentioning human rights in the constitution or declaring human right as universal is enough to realise its value or not. What else should we do in terms of implementing human rights at the grassroots level? How can we educate people towards human rights? These types of problems we often face in third world countries where illiteracy, ignorance, and other social practices come as social cleavages in the way of achieving human rights. Through Human rights education, we can attain this goal. However, introducing human rights as a subject in the curriculum could be an appreciable step of government. But, what about those people who even don't have access to school. How can we bring them to school? Therefore, besides government institutions, associations like civil society should have to come forward to accomplishing this task. It encourages self directing learning style. It carries liberal approach which advocates individual rights as its basic tenet. Therefore, knowledge of human rights is necessary to its recognition.

Universal Declaration of Human Rights (UDHR)

As an aftermath of Second World War, human society felt the importance of human rights and freedom. Since, both world wars one and two had not only devastating effects on past society but also on future generations. Therefore, United Nation with the contribution of member states in the formation of draft for human rights, proclaimed the Universal Declaration of Human Rights on 10th December 1948. It was adopted by the UN General Assembly. This declaration embodies thirty articles on human rights. After this declaration, it sets the universal common standard of human rights. And, Member states include human rights in their national constitutions.

What are Human Rights?

Human rights are essential attributes of all human beings to lead a humanly life with dignity. In that order human rights belong to all human beings regardless of their differences. These rights are all interrelated, interdependent and indivisible. Universal human rights are often expressed and guaranteed by law, in the forms of treaties, customary international law, general principles and other sources of international law. International human rights law lays down obligations of governments to act in certain ways or to refrain from certain acts, in order to promote and protect human rights and fundamental freedoms of individuals or groups.

Human rights according to UDHR have some characteristics such as they are universal, inalienable, interdependent and indivisible equal, and non-discriminatory. Moreover, they are both rights and obligation.

Human Rights Education (HRE)

UDHR (Universal Declaration of Human Rights) urged member states to implement human rights value in community through human right education. World conference on human rights in Vienna in 1993 perceived human rights education as an "essential for the promotion and achievement of stable and harmonious relations among communities and for fostering mutual understanding, tolerance and peace" (Vienna Declaration). In response to an appeal by this World Conference, the General Assembly proclaimed the period 1995 to 2004 the UN Decade for Human Rights Education. The Delors Commission on Education for the Twenty-first Century was established by UNESCO in 1993 to define the emerging orientations of education policy, setting-out four basic pillars of learning essential for the future of education: "Learning to know"; "Learning to do"; "Learning to live together"; and "Learning to be".

Human rights education has been defined as education, training and information aimed at building a universal culture of human rights. A comprehensive education in human rights not only provides knowledge about human rights and the mechanisms that protect them, but also imparts the skills needed to promote, defend and apply human rights in daily life. Education for democratic citizenship focuses on educational practices and activities designed to help young people and adults to play an active part in democratic life and exercise their rights and responsibilities in society. Education for mutual respect and understanding highlights self-respect, respect for others, and the improvement of relationship between people of differing cultural traditions (UNESCO).

Even on 10 December 2004, UN General Assembly prepared the plan of action in the implementation of human rights for 2004-09 periods. It is called the first phase of HRE achievements which focussed on primary and secondary education. Second phase starts from 2010-14, which focused on higher education and human rights training for educators and all government officials. Currently, a third phase (2015-19) of world programme of HRE is committed to focus on consolidating the plan of action of both phases and along with it diffuses human right education and training in the sector of media professionals and journalists.

UNESCO plays its key role in human rights education by supporting "education for all" movement and assisting its member states to consider human right education in formulation of policy and programme.

Human rights education is an attempt to create a global culture of human rights in the world. For that recently, OHCHR (Office of the High Commissioner for Human Rights) incorporates with civil society as its contribution in strong realisation of human rights. OHCHR Executive Direction and Management Branch established civil society unit which gives civil society opportunity to work with OHCHR. This unit provides them broad information and advices on various human rights issues. Civil society is accessible to individuals to lodge a complaint on human rights violation. Even, civil society as third party plays an important role to submit complaint on the victim's behalf with their consent. Civil society is considered as a realm of freedom and could be the best place for promoting human rights.

In December 2011, the General Assembly adopted, without a vote, the United Nation Declaration on Human Rights Education and Training. The Declaration states that human rights education provides persons with knowledge and skills and develops their attitudes and behaviour so as to empower them to enjoy and exercise their rights, and to respect and uphold the rights of others (Art. 2). It affirms that States, and where applicable relevant governmental authorities, have the primary responsibility to promote and ensure human rights education and training, and that States should create a safe and enabling environment for the engagement of civil society and other relevant stakeholders in those processes (Art. 7).

Civil Society and Human Rights

Civil society has been a difficult term to define it in one single statement on which consensus could be made. Though, it is not a new phenomenon as idea but it gained academic attention during revival of this conception in the end of 19th century. Civil society presents only one aspect of social life not whole of it as society consists of family, economy, politics and many others. Therefore, society is expressed in much broader sense than civil society (Mohinder Singh, 2008).

Here are these two definitions of civil society:

> According to John Keane, "The emerging consensus that civil society is a realm of freedom correctly highlights its basic value as a condition of democracy; where there is no civil society there cannot be citizens with capacities to choose their identities, entitlements and duties within a political, legal framework." (John Keane, 1998)
>
> According to USAID, "Civil society is the term that best describes the non-governmental, not for profit, independent nature of organisations that allow for broad citizen partnership. The hallmark of a democratic society is the freedom of individuals to associate with like minded individuals, express their views publicly, openly debate public policy, and petition their government. Civil society organisations include human rights groups, professional associations, religious institutions, pro-democracy groups, environmental activist organisations, business associations, labour unions, media organisations, and voluntary association of people seeking to work for the public good." (V.S. Gupta)

Civil society promotes bottom-up approach in theory and practice. Bottom up approach in human rights education could be effective to involve peoples' participation from the grass-root level. This approach encourages different interest groups, groups association and local people's participation in decision making for the accomplishment of any project related to public good. Through this approach, decisions are taken on the basis of negotiations, healthy dialogues and consensus among people. Civil society develops skills and attitudes in their participants to make intercultural dialogue among people.

Relationship between Civil Society in History and Theory

Classical Theory

Civil society is a much debated term. It has been defined differently by various thinkers. First, this term has been conceptualised in Aristotle' thought on political society and also it appears in Cicero's ideas on *societas civilis*. Both political thinkers gave philosophical understanding of civil society in their perspective of rights. Though, they understood civil society as political society very narrowly confined with civil and political rights of citizens only, however, it gave the idea of achieving good life through using their rights as civic virtue in political community. In Greek and Roman periods, rights were protected by civic participation and upheld democratic value. Thus, classical political theory focused on making society ideal and just by citizen's participation in decision-making process.

Hobbes, John Locke, Rousseau are thinkers of social contract and natural rights theory, who contributed to suggest how could natural rights be ensured in the best way. Along with they leave the space further open in political theory to have discussion on rights. In Hobbes's thought, rights could be best nurtured and experienced in the presence of sovereign authority. Because, in the absence of it, society again would go back into state of nature which was considered according to Hobbes, a state of war. On the contrary, according to John Locke in state of nature, humans used to do their work according to their reason and law of nature. But as society attained some development and brought the concept of money in society it created problem for human beings. Property became cause of conflicts and inequality among people. Here, civil society came into existence through social contract for protecting individual's rights from this state of nature which after introducing of money had become place of conflicts. In that nature of state human's natural rights were not safe at all. Thus, here, civil society works as checks and balances on governments and also has right to go against the despotic nature of governments. For Locke, natural rights refer to life, liberty and property and only in presence of civil society people can enjoy their rights. He sees civil society as guardian of natural rights and freedom. Rousseau presented a different form of social contract theory and understood political rights of people as medium of expressing general will. And, in civil society, people by following their reason could live, free and preserve their rights. Here, he focuses that people must obey rule of law or supreme authority as it constitutes general will of people themselves. Therefore, they cannot disobey laws, and in that order, and society can achieve common good for all. Active participation in civil society would develop civic virtue and self-development of individual.

Scottish Enlightenment Theory

Industrial revolution made political theorists think on economic aspects of human life. It gave more importance to economical and moral rights of people than political rights. We have seen how classical theorists endorsed political right of people for their development and neglected economical rights. But, after emergence of capitalist society, people had started to find such mediator space where they could do free commerce activity. Therefore, Scottish Enlighten theory emerged in response of these developments. Scottish philosophers such as David Hume, Adam Smith, and Adam Ferguson emphasized on autonomous economic sphere from politics. Economic and moral right could be well pursued in civil society. Hence, this sphere of civil society is situated between state and family. By this point we could identify how rights regarding having property and making associations became significant for human progress.

Thus, we can say that in this period civil society evolved as market society or commercial society, where everyone would realize his freedom and rights through getting equal platform. Scottish moralists understood civil society as a source of ethics, where norms emerged from people rather than from external institutions such as a monarch or church. Undoubtedly, these thoughts, challenged the monarchy and superiority of church and gave thought of liberal democracy.

Contemporary Theory

Contemporary theorists such as Michael Walzer, Robert Putnam, Tocqueville describe civil society as a third sphere of civic engagement which is autonomous and separate from state and economy both. These theorists clearly demarcated this sphere from politics and economy, however, people's participation in association would deviously reinforce economic development and strengthen political, cultural development as well. It is considered as public sphere where social capital and generalized trust take place. It is closely related to human rights too, as it works as a means to realize individual's rights in respect of others rights and nurture ethics and values in society. People participate in associations which makes them competent in society.

After the collapse of USSR and end of cold war, the world witnessed third wave of globalization in all spheres of life. And neoliberal policy became a mantra for development. New nation states were emerging and democratization process was taking place in east European countries for instance, Poland, Czechoslovakia, where civil society played an important role for raising people's voice against authoritarian regime and demand for their rights. It was the revival of civil society. On the contrary, due to globalization process, third world countries have been facing many challenges like poverty, illiteracy, inequity and exploitation of human right. So neoliberal policy could be understood as elitist model of development excludes large sections of society. Technological and industrial development creates middle class in society. Along with, new social movements come forward and challenge existing development model and demand for alternative development for developing nation. Alternative development includes humanistic approach which measures development in terms of human capability. Indian economist Amartya Sen and Pakistani Mahbub ul Haq gave new method of Human Development Index that consists of life expectancy at birth, education and decent standard of living.

Thus, NGOs, civic association, new social movements have alliance with international organizations and they are creating awareness and educating people towards human rights. Civil society as promoter of human right, works as mediator of society to reach its voice to the system and always stands by people for justice. It tries to make horizontal relation among community and strengthen participation at grass-roots level, Kerala state of India sets great example of developed civil society and consolidated democracy despite having ethnic community in region. It affirms that civil society through its attributes like social capital, trust, norms, and civic engagement brings solidarity and human ethics in society.

Recently, OHCHR collaborates with civil society as its contribution in strong realisation of human rights. OHCHR Executive Direction and Management Branch established civil society unit which gives civil society opportunity to work with OHCHR. This unit provides them broad information and advice on various human rights issues. Civil society is accessible to individuals to lodge complaint for human rights violation. Even civil society as third party also plays important role to submit complaint on their behalf with the consent of individuals.

Challenges

Multiculturalism, diversity and pluralism are the issues coming in the way of implementation of human rights education. How minority rights could be well addressed in human rights education? We know, both rights are opposite to each other. Human rights focus on individual's rights which are universal while minority rights focus on group rights that vary from one society to another society. Here, due to group differentiated rights, it leaves the space open for those bad and inhuman social practices which need to be eradicated. "The issue of the treatment of minorities within minorities has itself become the subject of considerable debate, many arguing that respect for minorities cannot become grounds for accepting mistreatment of internal minorities" (Chandran Kukathas, 256). Therefore sometimes principle of human rights encounter with group rights. According to Will Kymlika, "minority rights could not simply be subsumed under human rights because human rights standards are simply unable to resolve some of the most important and controversial questions relating to cultural minorities" (Chandran Kukathas, 251).

Other communitarians and feminists also challenge and criticize human rights by saying that there are individual rights which are created by individual males in attempt of maintaining their position in society. They opposed these theories on the basis of biases towards community, women and marginal groups. Here, civil society could play important role in bridging gaps between diverse communities. Ashutosh Varshney advocates that civic ties in multiethnic societies like India could prevent ethnic violence and disputes. So problem of multicultural society in relation to human rights could be well sorted out through civic engagement.

In a multicultural society, social integration is established by shared liberal political values. Civil society will provide both arena for finding common grounds, and integrative and collaborative modes of action. In fact, civil society mediates between government and the private sector, and helps conflicting institutions and belief system to evolve mutually acceptable formula for operation. In this sense, civil society also helps to resolve the contradictions that a democratic state may generate or encounter in the course of its operation (Nayar, 2001).

Conclusion

In context of human rights education, civil society has significant role for imparting human rights values in society as it was noticed how civil society has been active in terms of defending rights and liberty of individual. In ancient Greek and Roman period, we have seen how political and civil rights were given to citizens. After that in 17th century, Locke developed concept of civil society as a standard of measuring political order of that time. This civil society provides such laws and common judgement that protect and preserve life, liberty and property of individual. It shows Locke's concept of civil society which gives his subjects rights to revolt and challenge against absolute political system. Here, basic fundamental human rights are protected through civil society. Scottish enlightenment thinkers see civil society's sphere as an economic sphere where individuals can pursue their self-interest in market without any interference of state. These economic rights of people encouraged them to do their economic practices autonomously. And, since then civil society has been an autonomous place based on moral foundation where people use their rights and educate others as well. Civil society always fought for these rights like civil, political, social, cultural and now is fighting for third generation rights. However, there is also a need to address those challenges posed by communitarians, multiculturalists and feminists for making human rights significant, as Gandhi, who talks about self-reliant people through giving rights to people. And, in this regard civil society is not only making people aware towards human rights but also to make them responsible to promote human rights among others. It helps to create society more humane and just. Thus, civil society by its attributes, like social capital, civic competence, and deliberation creates an environment which could inculcate human rights values in society. Since civil society represents its normative aspect very strongly that carries basic liberal features such as liberty, equality, justice and rights of people, it can urge the government to work at grass-root level, to which, human rights education hardly reaches out. So, government institution and civil society together can empower individuals towards their human rights, as human rights education is all about developing skills, knowledge, critical and rational thinking in relation to human rights.

REFERENCES

Gaus, Gerald F. and Kukathas, Chandran (2004). "Nationalism and Multiculturalism". In Gaus, Gerald F. and Kukathas, Chandran (eds). *Handbook of Political Theory*. Sage Publication.

Gupta, V.S. (2004). *Communication Development and Civil Society*, Concept Publishing Company. New Delhi.

http://www.humanrightseducation.info/images/stories/pdf/Compendum.pdf

http://www.ohchr.org/EN/Issues/Pages/WhatareHumanRights.aspx

Keane, John (1998). "Civil Society: Old Images", *New Visions*. Stanford University Press. p. 114.

Nayar, P.K.B. (2001). "Civil Society, State and Democracy: Lessons for India", In *Sociological Bulletin*, 50(2), pp. 212-13.

Singh, Mohinder (2008). "Civil Society". In Rajeev Bhargava and Ashok Acharya (eds). *Political Theory: An Introduction*, Dorling Kindersley India.

UNESCO (2011). "Contemporary Issues in Human Right Education". UNESCO Vienna Declaration and Programme of Action, Part I, pars 33-34 and Part II, pars. pp. 78-82.

3

Biomedical Research Ethics Involving Humans and Issues of Human Rights in India

(Observations from Violation of Informed Consent and Illegal Medical/Drug Experiments)

Subhendu K. Acharya, Pradipta K. Das and *Gautam K. Kshatriya*

> The ethical resistance of the powerless others to our capacity to exert power over them is therefore what imposes unenforceable obligations on us. The obligations are unenforceable precisely because of the other's lack of power. That actions are at once obligatory and at the same time unenforceable is what put them in the category of the ethical. Obligations that were enforced would, by the virtue of the force behind them, not be freely undertaken and would not be in the realm of the ethical. Hoy, D. (2005)
>
> (Critical resistance from poststructuralism to postcritique, Massachusetts Institute of Technology, Massachusetts, 2004, p. 184)
>
> It is dangerous to be right on matters on which those in power are wrong. Voltaire

Introduction: Need of Ethics and Human Rights

The attribute of being ethical is an outcome of bio-cultural evolution. It is furthered by cultural norms and social teaching to develop the attitude of fellow feeling among the individuals for a peaceful coexistence and to protect the rights of individuals, particularly the vulnerable and weaker sections of the society.

It is the worldview of the whole humanity through civilization, which has been inculcated in the process of time as per belief system.

In the evolutionary process of human civilization, the sociality led to the development of human societies against every odd during primitive time. Group living becoming inseparable character in human struggle for existence led to the evolution of band society. To keep the band together, certain normative principles were devised which later on were elaborated to develop morals and ethics.

Society not only ensured provision of food security to its members but also took care of the children, women and physically infirm. Kinship gave more strength to the society by introducing obligatory relationship. Altruistic behaviour was encouraged. Difference between 'right' and 'wrong', 'sin' and 'virtue, 'moral' and 'immoral' acts were defined by collective wisdom of the society, comprehensive and acceptable to all the members. As Henry Rink observed in his study among the Eskimos that any act or behaviour by any member of the band or society detrimental to the interest of other persons, by failure to observe them, brings upon the offender the contempt of the whole tribe, and he runs the risk of becoming an outcaste and of being banished from his clan. Otherwise, the offender might bring up the displeasure of the wronged animals, or of the spirits of the ancestors who protect the tribe (Henry Rink, 1887). Truthfulness is an essential virtue for the member leading group life under natural conditions. Morality was made infused into a person and made a part of 'conscience' or inner-self. Breach of morality is a 'sin' which goes against natural system. Any wilful or inadvertent violation of social rules constitutes offence.

As human mind developed through time, the societal structure and its management system became more complex. Experiences were piled up per generation, old rules were amended and new rules introduced. In all cases, the ultimate objective was to benefit most members and uphold personal dignity and rights of the members of the society.

In different areas of the earth, different environment prevailed, encouraging the human societies to frame rules appropriate to thrive in those conditions. Since, the rise of civilized societies, ethical principles were followed and those who flunked the accepted norms were 'barbarians'. Ethics dictated hunting practices and warfare. Ethics protected the natural rights of all, whether a friend or foeman or animal.

This sociality is the primary base of mutual respect, the basis of morality or in other sense, the human rights. With the appearance of religion, even in its crudest form, human ethics was enriched by a new element, which gave to that ethics certain stability. With further development of social life, the conception of rights and justice in mutual relations had to become more and more prominent. Justice is necessary in mutual relations and it had to be made by Man for the sake of the preservation of social life itself promoting the rights of the participants in the society. And truly, in any society the desires and the passions of individuals inevitably collide with the desires of the other members of the same society. Such collisions would inevitably lead to endless feuds and to disintegration of the society, if it were not that human beings develop a conception of the equality of right of all the members of the society.

Biomedical Ethics

The aspects of biomedical ethics were first perceived as 'Bioethics' in 1926 by Fritz Jahr in an article about the "bioethical imperative" (Rincic, I. and Muzur, A. 2012). Further, Rensselaer Potter used this term in 1970 in more broader sense by symbolizing solidarity towards the biosphere (Goldim, J. R., 2009). Bioethics or biomedical ethics in its present form is defined as the convention for the protection of human rights and dignity of the human being with regard to the application of biology and medicine. In the beginning, the great demand for medical ethics was grounded in reaction to some negative events, such as the research experiments on human subjects committed by the Nazis and the Tuskegee Syphilis Study (1932-72) in the USA. At that time, bioethics was rather driven by urgent cases and did not consider systematic problems in healthcare such as the access to quality care. However, in reaction to these horrible events, the Nuremberg Code (1947) and the Declaration of Helsinki (1964) were created in order to provide researchers and physicians with ethical guidelines (Internet Encyclopedia of Philosophy).

In Indian context, the guidelines by Indian Council of Medical research formulated the first Ethical guideline for biomedical research in February 1980. The guideline was further modified in the year 2002 and latest in the year 2006 (ICMR, 2006).

The general statement of the guidelines by ICMR is as follows:

"Medical and related research using human beings as research participants must necessarily ensure that—

- The PURPOSE, of such research is that it should be directed towards the increase of knowledge about the human condition in relation to its social and natural environment, mindful of that the human species is one of the many species in a planet in which the well being of all species is under threat, no less from the human species as any other, and that such research is for the betterment of all, especially the least advantaged.
- Such research is CONDUCTED under conditions that no person or persons become a mere means for the betterment of others and that human beings who are subject to any medical research or scientific experimentation are dealt with in a manner conducive to and consistent with their dignity and well being, under conditions of professional fair treatment and transparency; and after ensuring that the participant is placed at no greater risk other than such risk commensurate with the well being of the participant in question in the light of the object to the achieved.
- Such research must be subjected to a regime of EVALUATION at all stages of the proposal i.e., research design and experimentation, declaration of results and use of the results thereof, and that each such evaluation

shall bear in mind the objects to be achieved, the means by which they are sought to be achieved, the anticipated benefits and dangers, the potential uses and abuses of the experiment and its results, and above all, the premium that civilised society places on saving and ensuring the safety of each human life as an end in itself." (Director General, ICMR, 2006)

This guideline has set out following 12 fundamental principles:

- Principles of essentiality
- Principles of non-exploitation
- Principles of privacy and confidentiality
- Principles of voluntariness, informed consent and community agreement
- Principles of precaution and risk minimization
- Principles of professional competence
- Principles of accountability and transparency
- Principles of the maximisation of the public interest and of distributive justice
- Principles of institutional arrangements
- Principles of public domain
- Principles of totality of responsibility
- Principles of compliance

(Director General, ICMR, 2006)

Biomedical Ethics and Issues of Violation of Human Rights

The ever increasing power of modern medicine and the complex, sociological settings in which it is practiced raise new ethical questions concerning what is just, what is good, and what is right in the behaviour of doctors and patients, of individuals and of society (The UNESCO Chair in Bioethics). Innovations were made to flood the market with high yielding varieties of plants, animals and novel therapeutics like vaccines, enzyme concoctions and other drugs. Utilization of biomedical knowledge to help humanity is not a contested proposition.

UNESCO General conference on human rights and bioethics has put forth the view '...Recognizing that ethical issues raised by the rapid advances in science and their technological applications should be examined with due respect to the dignity of the human person and universal respect for, and observance of, human rights and fundamental freedoms' (UNESCO, 2005). The era of post world war II witnessed a rapid progress in human genetics and the recent years have seen the emergence of several sub-fields such as genetic epidemiology, anthropological genetics, human biochemical genetics, human cytogenetics, medical genetics, clinical genetics, behavioural genetics, molecular genetics, radiation genetics, genetic engineering and so on, having applications for the welfare of people. Human genetic research aims at understanding the mechanics of gene-environment interactions.

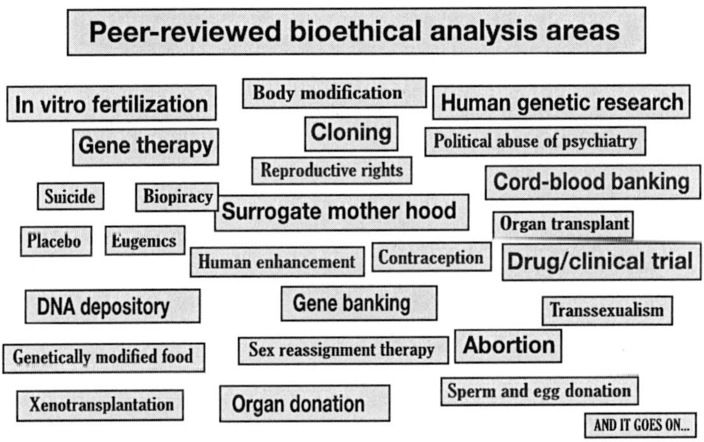

Going historically, the scenario changed after the end of cold war with break down of communist Soviet Union and re-unification of Germany. Globalization accelerated with a boom in information technology. Business alliances between the countries of the developed and developing world experienced a major boost. Populations from all over the world were now targeted as consumers. But the realization of one-medicine-does-not-fit-all was looming the dangers of such widespread targeting. The excitement attached with the novelty of gene therapeutics and drug therapies combined with the ease of market access in developing and underdeveloped nations lead to their widespread and at times reckless implementation. The sad aftermath was however a breakdown of the ethics associated with distribution of such products.

The Informed Consent

Informed Consent is defined as collecting the consent of the participant by providing him adequate information regarding the research in a simple and easily understandable unambiguous language.

Biomedical ethics aims to distinguish between research and treatment where the research participants take the drugs or undergo the procedures that fulfil the conditions of the experiment and not to benefit his or her health. So this voluntary dimension of the participant is necessary to be communicated to him or her and informed consent primarily serves this purpose. It is necessary to understand and consider socioeconomic contexts, material practices, and the ethicopolitical dynamics that define the very essence of informed consent.

The ICMR ethical guideline has recommended following 12 points as components of the consent form which were also highlighted in the UNESCO guidelines for bioethics and human rights:

1. Nature and purpose of study stating it as research
2. Duration of participation with number of participants
3. Procedures to be followed
4. Investigations, if any, to be performed
5. Foreseeable risks and discomforts adequately described and whether project involves more than minimal risk
6. Benefits to participant, community or medical profession as may be applicable
7. Policy on compensation
8. Availability of medical treatment for such injuries or risk management
9. Alternative treatments if available

10. Steps taken for ensuring confidentiality
11. No loss of benefits on withdrawal
12. Benefit sharing in the event of commercialization
13. Contact details of PI or local PI/Co-PI in multicentric studies for asking more information related to the research or in case of injury
14. Contact details of Chairman of the IEC for appeal against violation of rights
15. Voluntary participation
16. If test for genetics and HIV is to be done, counseling for consent for testing must be given as per national guidelines
17. Storage period of biological sample and related data with choice offered to participant regarding future use of sample, refusal for storage and receipt of its results.

Illegal Drug Trial and Human Rights Violation

Major pharmaceutical companies from around the world are conducting trials of their newly released drug on patients in underdeveloped and developing countries. Most of the Asian and African countries are the destination of such trials for these multinationals as the poor and less informed patients of such countries are being posed as guinea pigs. The loosely structured drug regulatory system allows such practices. Certain incentive-hungry physicians are prescribing such drug applications practices and simultaneously are reporting the results to the respective pharmaceuticals. Particularly the very poor monitoring of 'adverse drug reactions' (ADR) is a matter of serious concerns. It is highly unethical on the part of drug producers and immoral for doctors to use ignorant poor patients as experimental subjects. The issues of sufferings, deformities and deaths of these powerless people are not being addressed at all or are addressed partially. The guidelines of biomedical ethics have remained as simple formalities.

There are going on many such medical trials and experiments where the consent of the subject or his/her relatives was not taken. Few of the many such violation of human right during medical trials which were much publicized and highly criticized are worth mentioning here.

The case of illegal clinical trial of anti-cervical cancer in Andhra Pradesh and Gujarat

A serious issue of illegal clinical trial of an anti-cervical cancer vaccine came to the news in the year 2011 and was widely discussed and criticized in public forum. The documents show that large-scale clinical trial was conducted on 24,000, 10-14 years girls, mostly belonging from tribal community in Andhra Pradesh and Gujarat by MSD Pharmaceuticals Pvt. Ltd. and GlaxoSmithKline Ltd. With the help of an Indian NGO named PATH. Four of the 14,091 in Andhra Pradesh, two of the 10,686 in Gujarat died (G. Mudur, 2010). While company in the home page of its website has mentioned that the duration of protection of Gardasil, the tried vaccine has not been established. (http://www.gardasil.com/). This phase IV trial based on a study carried out on just 110 children by foreign pharmaceutical companies not registered in India. Indian Council of Medical Research "provided technical support for the development of protocols and advised on ethical issues". While ICMR first denied the deaths due to illegal trials, violation of Indian biomedical ethics guidelines was observed by the expert committee later and was confirmed by Union Health Minister.

The case of drugs trial in Regional Cancer Centre in Thiruvananthapuram, Kerala

The RCC's "collaborative venture" with the U.S.-based Johns Hopkins University (JHU) to test the effectiveness of certain chemicals as anti-cancer drugs seemed to have the ubiquitous flaw, right from the beginning: it failed to address the primary duty of preventing the abuse of research subjects with or without their knowledge (*Frontline*, 2001). It was claimed that an investigational drug was injected into cancer patients at the Regional Cancer Centre (RCC) in Thiruvananthapuram, the state capital, without clearance from the Drug Controller

General of India, and without approval from the institutional ethical committee (K.S. Jayaraman, 2001).

Illegal drugs trial on Industrial gas leak disaster

Bhopal a central Indian city witnessed one of the worst industrial disasters of the world in 1984 from a deadly gas leak killing about 20,000 and leaving many more incapacitated. About 30 years suffering from the happening of this tragedy, the illegal drugs trial came to these survivors as a new disaster at personal as well as emotional level that these people have been again put to an illegal drugs trial. It was revealed that a number of drugs under trial were administered on the patients without the informed consent or under reduced autonomy in Bhopal Memorial Hospital and Research Centre (BMHRC) and out of 279 people under the trial, 215 were gas survivors while the further report says at least 10 gas victims died while they were on these drug trials. As per the inspection report by Central Drugs Standard Control Organization (CDSCO), out of 26 clinical trials conducted in this hospital, 23 trials had irregularities by violating good medical practice norms.

The Case of Rebati, A Khondh Girl

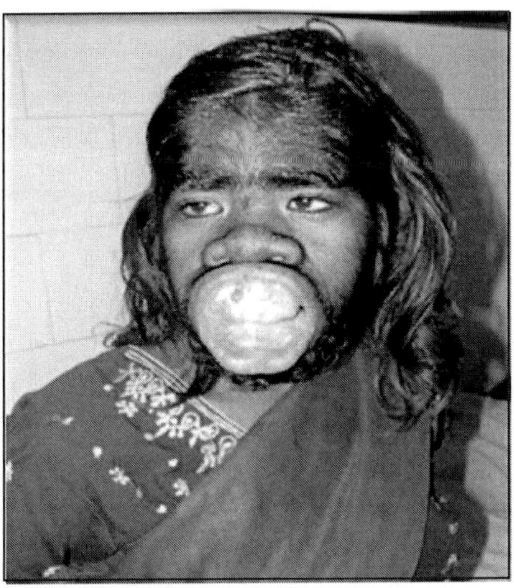

The plight of a Khondh girl, Rebati came to the public domain of scrutiny in 2008. Rebati was first reported in local news papers about her physical abnormalities. In SCB medical college and hospital, at Cuttack in Odisha this 13 year old girl suffering from inherited genetic disorder Idiopathic gingival enlargement (swelling of the gums) with hypertrichosis (abnormal growth of hair) was admitted. At first, the doctor at SCB medical college and hospital declared as a serious dental disease. A surgery was done as an experiment without proper investigation on the abnormalities. Rebati became a subject of curiosity and an avenue of experiment. As *The Hindu* reported a Staff nurse stole blood sample, telling the father of the girl that the blood sample was for further test. The accused Nurse latter admitted that one Professor from another Department told her to do so (*The Hindu*, 2008). The incident happened in July 2008 and a police case was registered which had no outcome.

Clinical Trials | Market India vs. Global: Growth Rates

- Newest data: 7% of all Phase III and 3% of studies globally are conducted in India
- India in top 15 countries, and may be considered an established force in CTs

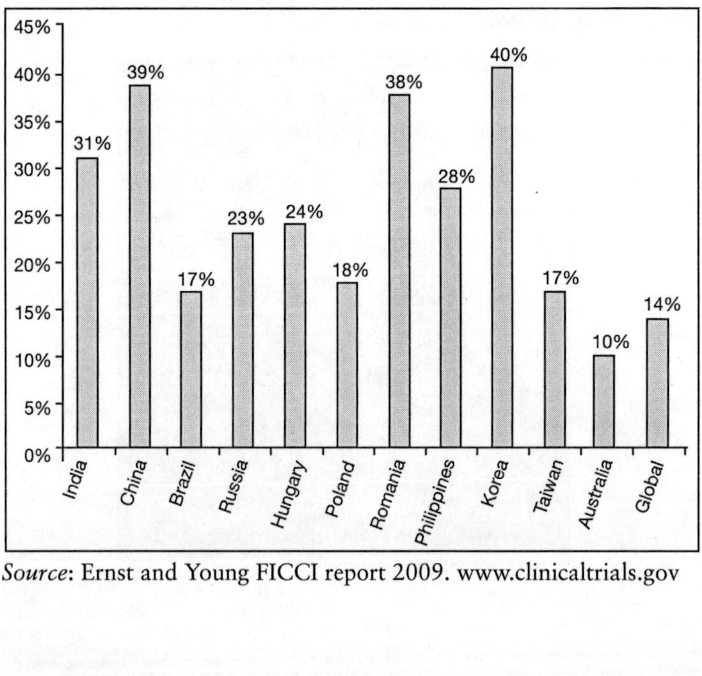

Source: Ernst and Young FICCI report 2009. www.clinicaltrials.gov

It is clearly visible from the above cited cases that doctors no more bear the humanist within, rather than becoming the messengers of market driven capitalist society. India is turning into a hot destination for drug trials where patients are being administered the trial drugs or vaccines many a times without their consents, being treated as guinea pigs.

India has several advantages as a host for such trials. Its biggest asset is probably the size of its population at more than 1 billion. In addition, Indians are increasingly suffering from the same illnesses as Americans and Europeans—diseases for which companies are desperate to find cures. For instance, at least 70 million Indians suffer from heart disease and 35 million have diabetes. It also has the edge over most developing countries because of its sophisticated hospitals and because many of its medical personnel speak English (T.V. Padma, 2005).

In a writ petition in Supreme Court of India filed by Swasthya Adhikar Manch (SAM) it was stated that the Ministry of Health and Family Welfare has not given complete information about 17778 (3458 deaths and 14320 Seriously Adverse Effects (SAEs)) which has taken place from January 2005 to December 2013 except stating that in 89 cases compensation has been paid. The Ministry has, however, not disclosed the names of persons who have died and to whom compensation has been paid. Between January 2005 to December 2013, 14320 SAEs and 3458 death have occurred, but no particulars of persons have been provided. The Ministry has also not given any detail of payment of compensation paid to the SAEs. The MOHFW has contended that there were no rules regarding compensation, therefore compensation has not been paid (Press Note. Swasthya Adhikar Manch, 2015).

In the past seven years, nearly 2,000 trials have taken place in the country and the number of deaths increased from 288 in 2008 to 637 in 2009 to 668 in 2010, before falling to 438 deaths in 2011, the latest figures available. In March 2013, the Indian health minister Ghulam Nabi Azad testified in the Rajya Sabha, the upper house of parliament, that the government has found that between 2005 and 2012, over 2868 deaths were recorded during government approved clinical trials of new drugs, 89 of which have been directly linked to the trials. To put this in context, Ken Getz, founder of the Centre for Information and Study of Clinical Research Participation in Boston says the global risk of dying in a clinical trial is 1 in 10,000. In India, the risk in 2011 was an order of magnitude higher (Laasya Sahmita, 2013).

But this whole issue raises serious ethical questions related to human rights. UNESCO in the Article 3 on Human dignity and human rights in its universal declaration on bioethics and human rights declares (1) Human dignity, human rights and fundamental freedoms are to be fully respected, (2) The interests and welfare of the individual should have priority over the sole interest of science or society (UNESCO, 2005).

Did the producers of this drug and their field partners declare the full range of possible side effects? Did the parents of these minors involved give "informed" consent? What is the criterion on which the target population for the vaccine was selected? And are there sufficient screening mechanisms in place to report and check on any "adverse events" or side effects?

Role of Media and Civil Society in Maintenance of Bioethics and Human Rights

Indian population is highly heterogeneous with rich bio-cultural diversity. UNESCO in its declaration has emphasized that cultural diversity, as a source of exchange, innovation and creativity, is necessary to humankind and, in this sense, is the common heritage of humanity, but emphasizing that it may not be invoked at the expense of human rights and fundamental freedoms, while a person's identity includes biological, psychological, social, cultural and spiritual dimensions (UNESCO, 2005). Media has a very important and active role in addressing human rights issues both at individual and society level by highlighting such violation in the biomedical sector in society through its direct reach in diverse cultural background of Indian society. Media can successfully educate public by highlighting particular issues in biomedical ethics in relation to present scenario. Similarly the role of civil societies is crucial to bring a sustainable reform in that respect. For example, in certain western countries, continuous investigative news are found coming up in leading dailies, and reviews are conducted by different NGOs and public forums with respect to different drugs, starting from its trial, complicacies, success rate during trial, results, pros and cons of the drug, company's role and strategy for the marketing, etc. it is also a fact that everything does not go fare always. But none of these two agencies with respect to Asian continent have been found of being critical in this regard. Many a times media gets engaged in adopting the perspective from health and political-economic point of view while civil societies stand far away to take any stand on the issue. Lack of knowledge and training about such objectives, or failure to identify such public interests and human perspective, or any other, whatever may be the causes but this silence is putting tremendous impacts on common man's life. At the same time, different economic factors, rapidly changing and market driven society, effect of globalization, rapid industrialization, etc. might be making their presence felt strongly being the compelling dynamics, but it is also another realization of the present time that there has been a great fall in social and human ethics in such countries.

Importance of Teaching in Biomedical Ethics to Maintain Human Rights

Teaching ethics and the normative pattern of a society for ethics to be functional, as it seems, is the only possible way to instil this trait among public. It is applicable to all form of ethics in the society throughout the world. In India, members of the biomedical research community have little knowledge of what biomedical ethics is, its guidelines, formulation procedure, the structure and construct of the ethical committee or the implementation of the guidelines. Getting approval for research projects and publishing papers, particularly in international journals is the prerogative of getting informed consent of participants or forming an institutional ethical committee. Neither any proper review nor any reform is being taken either at departmental ethical committee or central ethical committee level. UNESCO in its Article 23 on Bioethics education, training and information has laid out two important aspects, (1) In order to promote the principles set out in this Declaration and to achieve a better understanding of the ethical implications of scientific and technological developments, in particular for young people, States should endeavor to foster bioethics education and training at all levels as well as to encourage information and knowledge dissemination programmes about bioethics. (2) States should encourage the participation of international and regional intergovernmental organizations and international, regional and national non-governmental organizations in this endeavor (UNESCO, 2005). Technically, the concept of biomedical ethics exists in a very raw or crude form among most scientists and research scholars. It is a contrasting scenario in India to see that while the essence of the Indian society lives with high dependency on social morals and ethical constructions, while the civilization through its history has defended human rights, there is a very weak foundation with respect to biomedical ethics. So the big question is if the age old tradition of teaching humanism lacks in this front.

'The Speaking Tree' concept in Atharva Veda

The Indian teaching tradition is based on the preamble remembering the ethical and human right angle in mind with rich text in this respect. As it has been explained in Vedic literature, the knowledge of nature is not only an output of experiment by trial and error method. It is further explained that in order to use or to know the usefulness of any part of a plant, one has to address the plant and then to appease it. The plant being pleased gives away its own part and disseminates the knowledge about the medical utility of the parts along with the method of preparation. Such moral teaching has tremendous implication in present time.

Along with a proper legislative framework; its correct application; and adequate ethics training for professionals involved in research with human beings, are all key factors to ensuring the protection and promotion of human rights, safety and the well being of research participants all around the world (Building capacity to enhance ethics and human rights protection of participants in biomedical research, UNICRI, United Nations, Interregional Crime and Justice Research Institute). On the whole, it is necessary to strengthening institutional ethics committees and training the research fraternity to bring in an ethical tradition and to preserve the rights of the weaker sections.

REFERENCES

Bioethics. Internet Encyclopedia of Philosophy, available at (http://www.iep.utm.edu/bioethic/#SH2a, accessed on 10th January 2015).

Building capacity to enhance ethics and human rights protection of participants in biomedical research, UNICRI, United Nations, Interregional Crime and Justice Research Institute.

CBI probe to rebate case demanded. *The Hindu*; July 21, 2008.

Hoy, D. 2005. Critical resistance from poststructuralism to postcritique, Massachusetts Institute of Technology, Massachusetts, 2004, p. 184.

Director General, ICMR. 2006. Ethical guidelines for biomedical researches on human participants: ICMR, 2006. available at www.icmr.nic.in

FICCI and Earnst & Young Report. 2009. Compelling Reasons for Doing Clinical Research in India. available on www.clinicaltrials.gov.

Mudur, G. 2010. Human papillomavirus vaccine project stirs controversy in India. BMJ;340:c1775

Rink, Henry. *The Eskimo Tribes: Their Distribution and Characteristics, Especially in Regard to Language*. London. 1887.

Home page. http://www.gardasil.com/ accessed during March 2012.

Rincic, I. and A. Muzur. 2012. Fritz Jahr i ra anje europske bioetike (Fritz Jahr and the Birth of European Bioethics). Zagreb: Pergamena, p. 141.

Goldim, J.R. 2009. Revisiting the beginning of bioethics: The contributions of Fritz Jahr (1927). Perspect Biol Med, Sum, 377-380.

Jayaraman, K.S. 2001. Johns Hopkins embroiled in fresh misconduct allegations. Nature. 412-66: 2 August 2001.

Sahmita, Laasya. 2013. Badly run trials behind Indian drug testing freeze. New Scientist, 17th October 2013.

Misuse of science. *Frontline*: 18-17: Aug 17-31, 2001.

Press Note. 2015. India: Health Ministry Has No Records for the 475 Clinical trials in Ongoing Case of Illegal Drug Trials in the Supreme Court. Swasthya Adhikar Manch: Jan 2015. Available on [http://www.unethicalclinicaltrial.org]

Padma, T.V. 2005. India's drug test. Nature. 436-85: 28 July 2005.

The UNESCO Chair in Bioethics. 2005. Israel National Commission for UNESCO. Informed Consent. The International Center for Health, Law and Ethics, University of Haifa, Israel: October 2005.

UNESCO. 2005. Universal Declaration on Bioethics and Human Rights.

4

Human Rights Framework and Gender Equity: Need for a Genderquake

Bulbul Dhar James

Challenging Existing Power Equations

With culture and society providing the code of conduct, roles, challenges and opportunities for the societies to unfold in new directions and most significantly the space and boundaries within which to function; the 21st century has been a century of dramatic changes, with pulls and pushes of transformation, influencing the conventional roles of not just women but simultaneously of men, as well. In seeking empowerment, the existing power relations are being challenged, towards gaining greater control over the sources of power. The roles of sex (biologically determined, universal, given, unchanging with roles associated with reproduction) and gender (socially constructed, acquired, complex cultural elements associated with it), varies both within culture and in different cultures. These are assigned to individuals on the basis of socially determined characteristics, e.g. stereotypes, ideologies, values, attitudes, beliefs and practices. The very challenges and opportunities for the societies to unfold in new directions is a constant and herein the power dynamics are negotiated, subverted, challenged.

The process of challenging existing power relations and of gaining greater control over the sources of power is empowerment. Central to empowerment is power which is a social relationship that determines access to, use of and control over the basic material and ideological resources in the society. Power is the ability to: get what one wants, influence others, to think, feel, act or believe in ways that further one's interest. The kinds of power are reflected in terms of:

- The Power TO: relates to having decision-making authority, power to solve problems. Can be creative and enabling.
- The Power OVER: relates either/or a relationship of domination or subordination, based on socially sanctioned threats of violence, intimidation.
- The Power WITH: involves people organised with a common purpose or understanding to achieve collective goals.
- The Power WITHIN: refers to self-confidence, self-awareness and assertiveness to act in order to influence and change.

Unequal Spaces and Gender Inequality

The patriarchal influence functions in terms of various forms of subtle and insidious controls exercised over women in myriad ways such as control over the body, mobility, wealth/property, health, education/employment, participation/decision making and even autonomy/self-esteem. These get translated into barriers to mobility and spaces that women inhibit and challenges (whether external or internal) that women face. Structurally, these factors reflect bias in recruitment and promotion, 'Pipeline theory', limited opportunities in leadership training, etc., culturally—socialization, cultural barriers (class and background), family responsibilities, time conflicts, lack of physical mobility and finally personal factors—limited career aspirations, low self-esteem/weak, feeling intimidated, reluctance to increase responsibility, conflict between affiliation and power. In essence, power is utilized in certain spaces that could be physical, economic, socio-cultural, political and mental.

The feminist social scientists have emphasized the significance of space as a source of power. And spaces vary for the professionals depending upon the scope and geography of the organization, institution and household. For instance, space in terms of allowing the person, the place, the freedom and the margin to do what she/he intends to do. This is of particular significance in intra-household dynamics, but could also be applied to any group constituted to achieve certain goals, like in a company, department or collaborative research project. Time-space acts as a key factor in facilitating women to combine waged/salaried work and domestic work. It is common for women to trade off higher wages and better job opportunities for greater proximity, resulting in shorter journeys to work, lower overall travel distances, and smaller activity spaces. The spatial nature and amount of the information exchanged through place-based arrangements of private links (friends, associates, family, neighbours), are instrumental in shaping the locational choices especially those that women make, reflects the size of their activity spaces.

In the 21st century, it was anticipated that sophisticated information technology would radically modify this to 'de-spatialization of interaction' (as predicted by the likes of Dale Spender, William Mitchell, McKenzie Wark amongst others) and redrawing the gendered contours of home and work. Nevertheless, what we seem to have today is a perpetuated, very gendered outcome for most women.

Criticality of Sex Segregation

In the construction and maintenance of gender disparity in the workplace, sex segregation plays a critical role. This is insidious and all-encompassing, influencing every facet and course of women's work lives limiting their goals, aspirations and options. Despite the 20th century, being a century of dramatic changes, with pulls and pushes of transformation, influencing the conventional roles of both men and women, the institution of PATRIARCHY remains as the underlying preconception. The transformation of men's and women's work-roles stands out among the many technological, economic, social and cultural changes in the last half of the twentieth century. But, despite this progress, inequality remains with men being more likely to have access to paid employment, to be employed in better jobs, and to be better paid in those jobs.

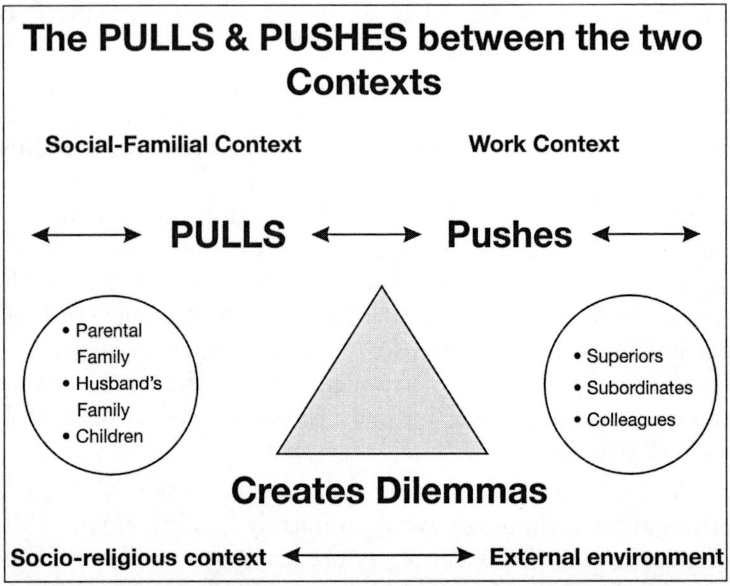

The Membership and Responsibility of the Women's Home and Work Interface reflecting the dilemma of ACTION CHOICES, Demands and Expectations—SUPPORTIVE & INHIBITIVE Processes, Designing PRIORITIES and GOALS, Articulating STRESS and CHALLENGES in managing the two systems, Identifying the CHOICES required to be a Professional person in both the above systems, Identifying and stating the PRICE to be paid in redefining relationships and Re designating new roles for the SELF.

Implications for Gender Equality is manifest in Career Processes and trends as Occupational Feminization, Management and authority, Gender gap in Earnings and some Principle tangible awards. The growth in workforce participation is also cited as a root cause for other changes in gender relations such as marital power, fertility patterns, and political representation.

Gender affects careers in a variety of Settings and is recognized as lynchpin of Gender Inequality at work, viz. what areas of opportunities have opened up to working women and what barriers remain?; why women have entered some occupations in large numbers?; what the consequences of feminization can be?; etc.

Women continue to bear a disproportionate share of the domestic workload and that this uneven division of labour in the home is implicated in divisions of labour in the paid workforce (primarily taking the form of gendered segregation). A sociological approach to gender inequality is a necessary complement to the economic perspective. The research on sex segregation varies from occupational sex segregation (1968 Gross), anthropological (1974 Rosaldo, Lamphere) to interdisciplinary (1976 Blaxall and Reagan).

SEX Segregation and GENDER Inequality:

The degree to which men and women

- Do different work
- Work in different sectors of the economy
- A link between a Gender Gap in earnings and workplace segregation
- Gender Differences in Authority—GLASS CEILING, etc...

The problem was not just leaving women out of analysis but the questions asked and measures used were designed to understand the situation of male bread winners. Gender inequality was/is not reducible to a social class as women and men can be in the same social class but have very different gender statuses or the fact that women, whether they live in rich, middle class or poor families are more economically vulnerable than their male counterparts.

Intersecting Sociology with Economics ; Intersecting Politics and Culture

From a sociological viewpoint, manifests a significant gender gap in earnings due to interrupted work experience of women, female-dominated fields pay less starting salary as well as subsequent salary growth in promotion, seniority rather than higher productivity accounts for the experience premium, low wages contribute to low labour force attachment among women, on the job experience of women lower, depends also on who pays the cost of training. Thus, the gender gap needs to be looked at beyond skills to other processes at work.

The efficiency for economists naturally erodes prejudices and cultural beliefs, sociologists point to employment systems as adaptable systems reflecting and determining prejudices of members of society. The politics within the workplace affects the productivity, morale and retention. The social control thesis' main concern is access of women to different positions, jobs, occupations...authority, the differential valuation of the male-dominated vs female-dominated work and the consequent Undervaluation of the women's work.

Developing Countries' Approaches and Policy for Women

Origin:

- Growth/Economic Development Model
- Original WID Approach

Stabilization and SAP

- Women's Eco Contribution to Development
- Associated with Equity

- **UN Decade for Women**
- Redistribution with Growth and Basic Needs

CONTEMPORARY

- MDG's—as the Current Approach to Gender and Development

Approaches to Gender Inequalities: Conceptualises women's empowerment the unequal power relations which blocked the women's ability to participate in, and help to influence the development processes.

Women's Empowerment Framework: The Longwe and Sushma Sahay identifies five levels of equality which indicate the extent to which women are equal with men, and have achieved empowerment: Welfare, Access, Conscientisation, Participation and Control. These levels are hierarchical (with control at the top); if an intervention focuses on the higher levels, the empowering effect is likely to be greater than if it focuses on the lower levels-welfare interventions are unlikely to be found empowering by women. Another dimension of the framework is the level of recognition of 'women's issues' an issue becomes a 'women's issue' when it looks at the relationship between women and men, rather than simply at women's traditional and subordinate sex-stereotyped gender roles (March et al., 1999). This deals with the extent to which the objectives are concerned with women's development, and to establish whether women's issues are ignored or recognised.

The framework develops the concept of practical and strategic gender needs into a progressive hierarchy, which depends on the extent to which an intervention has potential to 'empower'; and emphasises that empowerment is intrinsic to development (ILO, 1998). But the framework is static, ignoring changes over time; it fails to examine the institutions and organisations involved or the macro-environment; and by defining development only in terms of women's empowerment, it can tempt users to focus only on women rather than on gender relations or other forms of social difference.

Social Relations Approach, developed by Naila Kabeer, is a method for analysing gender inequalities regarding the distribution of resources, responsibilities and power, and for designing policies and programmes which enable women to be agents of their own development (March et al., 1999). Unlike the previous frameworks, this approach uses concepts rather than tools to analyse the relevant issues. Kabeer presents development as increasing human well-being, which concerns survival, security and autonomy. By expanding the concept of production, Kabeer forcefully challenges the undervaluing of non-market activities that occur in some frameworks, e.g. within households and argues that development interventions should support relationships that build on solidarity and reciprocity, and build autonomy, rather than reduce it (March et al., 1999). Social relations are dynamic structural relationships that create and reproduce systemic differences in the positioning of different groups of people, and determine our roles, responsibilities, claims, resources, and level of control. The argument is that poverty arises out of people's unequal social relations, which dictate unequal relations to resources, claims and responsibilities. It is also through social relations (for example, networks of family and friends) that many poor people survive. From a political economy perspective, the analysis of four key institutional location, viz. the state, the market, the community, and family/kinship the ideological neutrality and independence of institutions, is challenged.

Gender and Development Framework: The Moser Framework forms part of the GAD (Gender and Development) critique of the WID approach to development, and argues for an integrated gender-planning perspective in all-development work, concentrating on the power relations between men and women (Moser, 1993). The framework attempts to establish 'gender planning' as a type of planning in its own right, and questions the assumption that planning is a purely technical task (March et al., 1999). Moser identifies a 'triple role' for low-income women involving reproductive, productive and community—management activities (primarily an extension of women's reproductive role), compared to men's largely dual role of productive and community-politics activities (organised, formal politics, often within the framework of national politics). The recognition of women's triple role—with the aim of ensuring that tasks are equally valued—highlights work (community-management) that is often ignored in economic analysis. The second, gender needs assessment, is based on the concept that women (as a group) have particular needs that differ from men (as a group) as a consequence of both women's triple role, and their subordinate position to men in most societies.

The *practical gender needs* (*PGNs*) are largely practical in nature and their fulfilment will not challenge the existing gender division of labour or women's subordinate position in society.

Roles, Needs of Women (Developing Countries' Policy)

PGN (Practical Gender Needs)	**PGN**
• in **reproductive roles**	• in **productive roles**
• Food aid, family planning	• Earn income
	• Small scale Y generation
SGD (Strategic Gender Needs)	**Declining Social Services**
• State top down intervention	• All 3 of the above roles
• Pol-Eco autonomy	• Elasticity of women's time

The *strategic gender needs* (*SGNs*) exist because of women's subordinate social position, and are related to gender divisions of labour, power and control (*ibid.*). If met, SGNs would enable women to transform existing imbalances of power between men and women (for example, removal of institutionalised forms of discrimination, measures against male violence, etc.). When analysing other aspects of intra-household difference, the concept of women's triple role is significant; it makes visible all areas of work and helps promote reasonable valuing of work.

Capability Approach, cencept proposed by Amartya Sen emphasises a real freedoms that people have for leading a valuable life, that is, on their capabilities to undertake activities such as reading, working, or being politically active, or of enjoying positive states of being such as being healthy or literate. Sen has claimed that "the question of gender inequality...can be understood much better by comparing those things that intrinsically matter like functionings and capabilities, rather than just the means to achieve them like...resources. The issue of gender inequality is ultimately one of disparate freedoms" (Sen 1992: 125). The capability approach only provides a general framework and not a worked out *modus operandi* to study gender inequality.

Human Rights-based Approach: Unlike the above approaches, this conceptualises the multi-dimensional aspect of inequality in the context of caste-class-gender interconnections and hence we can address the exploitation, oppression and domination in the multiplicity of contradictions. It is a framework that integrates the norms, principles, standards and goals of the international human rights system into the plans and processes of development.

A vibrant aspect of the Human Rights-based Approach is about identifying root causes of poverty, empowering rights-holders to claim their rights, enabling duty-bearers to meet their obligations in the macro perspective of the re-emergence of the state and governance as a central element in development, through a focus on the interrelation between the state and its citizens in terms of duties and rights. It emphasises the basic obligation of the state to take care of its most vulnerable citizens, including those not able to claim their rights for themselves. Bina Agarwal argues that women need an improvement in their ability to pursue their interest, including strengthening their bargaining power (Agarwal 1998). She further argues that this strengthening would come from improving their fallback position.

The spotlight on empowerment, the connection to development is crucial and inclusive that includes beneficiaries, stakeholders and partners when deciding development strategies and goals, where participation is more than just a tool—it is also the goal for development, accountability is not only a concern for the outcome of development, but also for the process by which it is achieved and for the organisations implementing it and that development should promote platforms and networks for mobilisations and support people's ability to take part in governance and claim their rights individually and in groups.

> Gender equality is more than a goal in itself. It is a precondition for meeting the challenge of reducing poverty, promoting sustainable development and building good governance.
>
> *UN Secretary-General Kofi Annan*

The attention on equality between women and men is based on the proposition that equality is fundamental to human rights, and that it is a necessary for real and sustainable people-centric development. Gender equality can be explained in terms of equal rights, opportunities and obligations of men and women and increased empowerment manifest in the greater potential for both men and women to influence, participate and benefit from development processes.

The nature of the societal change and existence of gender equality are interconnected as women's empowerment and gender equity are at the centre of development objectives in its own right. Economic development is not enough to dissolve all gender disparities—what is needed is ongoing corrective measures addressing the continuing gender gaps. The macro-perspective is that more gender equality leads to greater productivity and more sustainable development. Women's access to employment and education opportunities reduces the likelihood of household poverty, and resources in women's hands have a range of positive outcomes for human capital and capabilities within the household.

Studies have shown that economic development on its own does not lead to gender equality. Indeed, some of the fastest growing developing countries show the least signs of progress on basic gender equality outcomes. Formal regular paid work has the greatest transformative potential for women, but this prospective has remained restricted because of the segmentation of labour markets. The World Development Report 2012 focuses on four priority areas for policy going forward: (i) reducing excess female mortality and closing education gaps where they remain, (ii) improving access to economic opportunities for women, (iii) increasing women's voice and agency in the household and in society, and (iv) limiting the reproduction of gender inequality across generations. The role of science and biotechnological changes is presented to women as an issue of "choice"—supposedly providing them greater control over the process and outcome—this is significant to monitor.

The lack of focus on inequality was a key limitation of the MDGs and, rightly, this has become a major priority for the post-2015 agenda. Empowerment slicing through the structural inequalities—women's economic empowerment through ensuring fairer access to productive resources and employment opportunities; women's political empowerment through ensuring greater representation in formal and informal decision-making positions in public and private sectors at local, national and international levels; and women's social empowerment by strengthening their capacity for collective voice and action through support for organisations dedicated to women's rights and gender justice is the need of the hour. At a more basic level strategic gender needs reflect challenge to the customary gender relations and imply changes in relationship of power and control between men and women. At the workplace women need to take responsibility for their mistakes and also for their successes. Policies invariably designed by men reflect masculine trends and tendencies—a space for catering to women's convictions and femininity are needed. Together men and women can give shape to new systems. Individually or singly systems became monolith or collapse.

Gender is not just one of many inequalities but the most persistent putting women at a disadvantage at every level of income and within every deprived faction, including caste, race and disability. Very similar to class inequalities in capitalist societies or caste inequalities structure India, gender too is structured into the social relations of production and reproduction of every possible society. In the duty that men and women take for the daily unpaid care work within the family and community, in their capability to marshal resources and access opportunities to contribute to family and community on both a paid and unpaid basis, and in the importance and recognition given to assistance rendered there is marked Inequality.

From a macro-perspective and considering the structural nature of gender inequality, meeting the development goals is of vital significance. Even from a CBA (cost-benefit analysis) perspective, it is clear that extensive benefits ensue to the society when gender equality is taken seriously—and conversely higher costs when it is not. A need to bring about a kind of 'genderquake' with an inclusive approach through gender audits and mainstreaming etc to correct the gender imbalance and inequity is of critical importance.

REFERENCES

Agarwal, Bina (1994) *A Field of One's Own, Gender, Land Rights in South Asia*, Cambridge University Press.

Kabeer, N. (1994) *Reversed Realities: Gender Hierarchies in Development Thought.*

Kabeer, N. (2012) "Women's economic empowerment and inclusive growth: Labour markets and enterprise development", SIG Working Paper 2012/1, SOAS, University of London, UK.

King, C. (2001) "Gender and Rural Community Development III: Tools and Frameworks for Gender Analysis", http://www.regional.org.au/au/apen/2001/p/KingC1.htm

Locke, C. and Okali, C. (1999) "Analyzing Changing Gender Relation: Methodological Challenges for Gender Planning". *Development in Practice*, Vol. 9, No. 3, pp. 274-86.

Longwe, S.H. (1991) "Gender Awareness: The Missing Element in the Third World Development Project". In Wallace, T. and Candida, M. (eds.) *Changing Perceptions: Writings on Gender and Development*. Oxfam.

March, C., Smyth, I. and Mukhopadhyay, M. (1999) *A Guide to Gender—Analysis Frameworks*. Oxfam.

Moser, C.O.N. (1993) *Gender Planning and Development: Theory, Practice and Training*. Rutledge.

Parekh Indira J. (2009) "Managing Personal and professional Goals", UGC, Capacity building for Women Managers in Higher Education.

World Development Report 2012, The World Bank, Washington DC.

5

Silent Revolution in Human Rights Education

Harsha Merchant

A silent revolution is happening through education since 2006. Several technical universities (including UP, Punjab, JNTU, Bhutan) have introduced a Foundation Course on Human Values and Professional Ethics, as an audit/credit course with amazing results. The teachers are trained through 8-day workshops and are the first to benefit. The course leads to self-discovery. It is about understanding harmony at all levels of human living; individual, family, society and with rest of existence. At SNDT Women University, Human Right Education course paper is also introduced as elective for B.Ed. programme. Efforts are on to introduce it in all educational institutions to empower people at the right stage of life. According to a report by Human Rights Watch, many countries have also failed to enact the convention that they have signed to. Let us summarize some of the common problems/issues children face, such as:

- Refugees (children make up over half of the world's refugees)
- Hazardous labour exploitation
- Physical abuse
- Sexual violence and exploitation
- Recruitment as child soldiers
- Police abuse and arbitrary detention of street children

- Orphans and abandoned children without adequate care
- Sexual abuse and trafficking
- Lack of access to education, or substandard education
- Corruption
- Violence
- Terrorism
- Over population.

Meaning of Human Rights

Human rights are rights, inherent to all human beings, whatever our nationality, place of residence, sex, national or ethnic origin, colour, religion, language, or any other status. We are all equally entitled to our human rights without discrimination. These rights are all interrelated, interdependent and indivisible.

Universal human rights are often expressed and guaranteed by law in the forms of treaties, customary international law, general principles and other sources of international law. International human rights law lays down obligations of Governments to act in certain ways or to refrain from certain acts, in order to promote and protect human rights and fundamental freedoms of individuals or groups.

Universal and Inalienable

The principle of universality of human rights is the cornerstone of international human rights law. This principle, as first emphasized in the Universal Declaration on Human Rights in 1948, has been reiterated in numerous international human rights conventions, declarations, and resolutions. The 1993 Vienna World Conference on Human Rights, for example, noted that it is the duty of States to promote and protect all human rights and fundamental freedoms, regardless of their political, economic and cultural systems. Human rights are inalienable. They should not be taken away, except in specific situations and according to due process. For example, the right to liberty may be restricted if a person is found guilty of a crime by a court of law.

Interdependent and Indivisible

All human rights are indivisible, whether they are civil and political rights, such as the right to life, equality before the law and freedom of expression; economic, social and cultural rights, such as the rights to work, social security and education, or collective rights, such as the rights to development and self-determination, are indivisible, interrelated and interdependent. The improvement of one's right facilitates advancement of the others. Likewise, the deprivation of one right adversely affects the others.

Equal and Non-discriminatory

Non-discrimination is a cross-cutting principle in international human rights law. The principle is present in all the major human rights treaties and provides the central theme of some of international human rights conventions such as the International Convention on the Elimination of All Forms of Racial Discrimination and the Convention on the Elimination of All Forms of Discrimination against women.

The principle applies to everyone in relation to all human rights and freedoms and it prohibits discrimination on the basis of a list of non-exhaustive categories such as sex, race, colour and so on. The principle of non-discrimination is complemented by the principle of equality, as stated in Article 1 of the Universal Declaration of Human Rights: "All human beings are born free and equal in dignity and rights."

Both Rights and Obligations

Human rights entail both rights and obligations. States assume obligations and duties under international law to respect, to protect and to fulfil human rights. The obligation to respect means that States must refrain from interfering with or curtailing the enjoyment of human rights. The obligation to protect requires States to protect individuals and groups against human rights abuses. The obligation to fulfil means that States must take positive action to facilitate the enjoyment of basic human rights. At the individual level, while we are entitled of our human rights, we should also respect the human rights of others.

Meaning of Education

By educating an individual, we attempt to give a person some desirable knowledge, understanding, skills, interests, attitudes and critical 'thinking'. That is, he/she acquires knowledge of history, geography, arithmetic, languages and sciences.

He/she develops some understanding about the deeper things in life, the complex human relations, and the cause and effect relationship and so on. He/she gets some skills in writing, speaking, calculating, drawing, operating some equipment etc. He/she develops some interests in and attitudes towards social work, democratic living, co-operative management and so on.

As an individual in the society, he/she has to think critically about various issues in life and take decisions about them being free from bias and prejudices, superstitions and blind beliefs. Thus, he has to learn all these qualities of head, hand and heart through the process of education.

ISSUES

Poverty

India suffers from substantial poverty. According to World Bank's estimates on poverty based on 2005 data, India has 456 million people, 41.6% of its population, living below the new international poverty line of $1.25 (PPP) per day. The World Bank further estimates that 33% of the global poor now reside in India. Moreover, India also has 828 million people, or 75.6% of the population living below $2 a day, compared to 72.2% for Sub-Saharan Africa. Official figures estimate that

27.5% of Indians lived below the national poverty line in 2004–2005. A 2007 report by the state-run National Commission for Enterprises in the Unorganized Sector (NCEUS) found that 25% of Indians, or 236 million people, lived on less than 20 rupees per day with most working in "informal labour sector with no job or social security, living in abject poverty".

Sanitation

Lack of proper sanitation is a major concern for the people of India. Statistics conducted by UNICEF have shown that only 31% of India's population is able to utilise proper sanitation facilities as of 2008. It is estimated that one in every ten deaths in India is linked to poor sanitation and hygiene. Diarrhoea is the single largest killer and accounts for one in every twenty deaths. Around 450,000 deaths were linked to diarrhoea alone in 2006, of which 88% were deaths of children below five. Studies by UNICEF have also shown that diseases resulting from poor sanitation affect children in their cognitive development.

Recognising the importance of proper sanitation, the Government of India started the Central Rural Sanitation Programme (CRSP) in 1986, in hope of improving the basic sanitation amenities of rural areas. This programme was later reviewed and, in 1999, the Total Sanitation Campaign (TSC) was launched. Programmes such as Individual Household Latrines (IHHL), School Sanitation and Hygiene Education (SSHE), Community Sanitary Complex, Anganwadi toilets were implemented under the TSC.

To meet this objective, incentives are given out to encourage participation from the rural population to construct their own sanitation amenities. In addition, the government has set out to educate its people on the importance and benefits of proper sanitation through mass communication and interpersonal communication techniques. This is done through mass and print media to reach out to a larger audience and through group discussions and games to better engage and interact with the individual.

Education

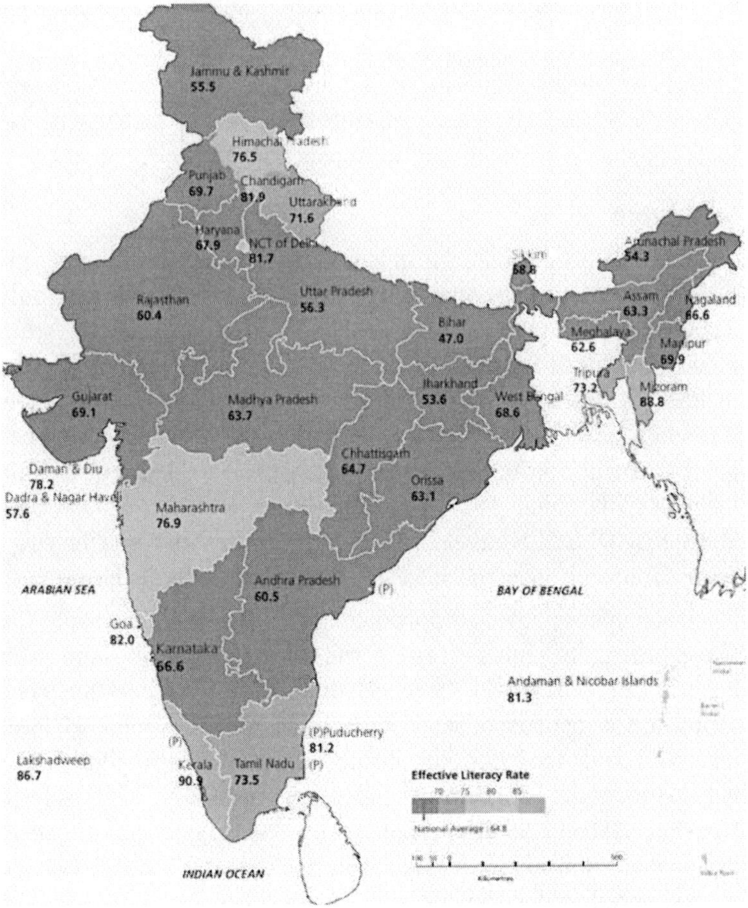

Literacy rate map of India, 2011

Initiatives

Since, the Indian Constitution was completed in 1949, education has remained one of the priorities of the Indian government. The first education minister Maulana Azad founded a system of education which aimed to provide free education at the primary level. Primary education was made free and compulsory for children from 6-14, and child labour was banned. The government introduced incentives to education and disincentives for not receiving education—for instance, the provision of mid-day meals in schools were introduced.

Many similar initiatives echoed, and the largest of such initiatives is Sarva Shiksha Abhiyan, which actively promoted "Education for All". In line with this, the United Progressive Alliance (UPA) aimed to increase their expenditure on education to 6% of its Gross Domestic Product (GDP) from values fluctuating about 3% through their National Common Minimum Programme (NCMP) in 2004. The Right of Children to Free and Compulsory Education Act was also imposed in 2009. Despite these initiatives, education continues to persist as an impediment to development.

While many schools were built, they had poor infrastructure and inadequate facilities. Schools in the rural areas were especially affected. According to District Information System for Education (DISE) in India in 2009, only about 51.5% of all schools in India have boundary walls, 16.65% have computers and 39% have electricity. Of which, only 6.47% of primary schools and 33.4% of upper primary schools have computers, and only 27.7% of primary schools have electricity. Learning in poorly furnished schools was not conducive, resulting in poor quality education.

Furthermore, the absence rates of teachers and students were high, while their retainment rates low. The incentives for going to school were not apparent, while punishment for absence was not enforced. Despite the government's decree on compulsory education and the child labour ban, many children were still missing classes to go to work. The government did not interfere even when children missed school.

Also, online country studies publications by the Federal Research Division of the Library of Congress stated that "it was not unusual for the teacher to be absent or even to subcontract the teaching work to unqualified substitutes". This exacerbates the problems of the lack of qualified teachers. Currently, the student-teacher ratio remains high at around 32, which is not much of an improvement since 2006 when the ratio was 34.

Economic and social disparities also plague the fundamentals of the education system. Rural children are less able to receive education because of greater opportunity costs, since rural children have to work to contribute to the family's income. According to the Annual Status of Education in 2009, the average attendance rate of students in the rural states is about 75%. Though, this rate varies significantly, states like Uttar Pradesh and Bihar had more than 40% absentees during a random visit to their schools. In the urban states, more than 90% of the students were present in their schools during a visit.

RTE Statistics in Maharashtra and Pune

- 31000 schools are running without teachers in Maharashtra (A study by Education Dept., GOM in 2010)
- 2.3 lakh of children were out of the school in the state. (by Education Dept., GOM in 2012)
- More than 50% Govt. schools are in lack of having facilities like infrastructure, sanitation, playground, drinking water etc. (district information education report 2011-12)

RTE Status in Maharashtra (2013-14)

Sl. No.	Division	Schools under the Act	Available RTE Seats	Vacant Seats	% of filled seats	% of vacant seats
1	Pune	1527	29019	13433	53.7	46.3
2	Mumbai	2240	44087	31376	28.8	71.2
3	Nashik	795	9006	3098	65.5	34.5
4	Amaravati	482	6892	1789	74.0	26
5	Nagpur	1040	10865	5136	52.7	47.3
6	Aurangabad	1209	11474	6467	43.6	56.4
7	Latur	1080	10927	7934	27.4	72.6
8	Kolhapur	1293	14297	6626	53.7	46.3
	Total	9666	136567	75859	44.4	55.6

(Data from Directorate of Primary Education, GOM—August 5, 2013)

RTE Admission Status (till July 17, 2014)

Sl. No.	District	Available RTE seats	Filled seats	Vacant Seats	% of filled seats	% of vacant seats
1	Ahmednagar	2832	1622	1210	53.74	46.26
2	Aurangabad	2435	179	2256	7.35	92.65
3	Beed	890	92	798	10.33	89.67
4	Kolhapur	1940	596	1344	35.97	64.03
5	Latur	1025	507	518	49.46	50.54
6	Mumbai	8223	1153	7070	14.02	85.98
7	Nashik	3665	1759	1906	47.99	52.01
8	Nanded	713	331	382	46.42	53.58
9	Nagpur	7411	3738	3673	50.43	49.57
10	Pune	13879	4665	9214	31.61	68.39
11	Solapur	4289	1482	2807	34.55	65.45
12	Satara	3554	1500	2054	42.20	57.8
13	Sangali	1640	639	1001	42.25	57.75
14	Washim	552	456	96	84.78	15.22
	Total	53048	18719	34329	39.36	60.64

(Data from Directorate of Primary Education, GOM, and Published in TOI Pune dated July 18, 2014)

Issues and Challenges for Admission under 25% Reservation

Parents/Guardians

- Hesitation in taking admission in reputed private schools—Some unknown fear, misconception, strong beliefs against such schools prevent them to apply and take admission of their ward.
- Illiteracy of the parents/guardian play major role in avoiding such schools. Lack of self-confidence, socially and economically backwardness, unknown about terms and conditions of RTE Act, lack of computer knowledge, non-availability of required documents and lack of follow up work may be the reasons for not utilizing this right.

School and Management

1. Not having clear idea about the Act.
2. Not accepting their application form and if accept, not issuing acknowledgement.
3. Demanding fees and also asking to pay for uniform, textbooks, computer training fees etc.
4. Demanding unnecessary documents.
5. Negative and discriminatory attitude of management and teachers towards these students and parents.

Government Officials

1. Unclear about the details of RTE.
2. Avoiding stakeholder's problems.
3. Not taking any strong actions against the concern schools.
4. Mismanagement.
5. No effect and use of grievance cell.
6. No commitment and no positive attitude towards implementation of RTE Act.

Technology

1. Lack of knowledge of the parents about "on line" admission.
2. Problems in scanning, uploading photo and documents.
3. Web site not updated.
4. No acknowledgement in on line admission.
5. Govt. help centers are not cooperative.
6. Lack of facilities in rural areas.
7. Problems in selection of school.
8. Issues regarding distance.

Suggestions to implement RTE (at individual/group level)

1. Writing articles in newspaper/magazine.
2. Preparing format of application to help parents to prepare application to school/govt.

3. Preparing videos/ppt based on RTE admission rules/ corporal punishment rules/examination and evaluation rules.
4. Helping parents to get necessary certificates for admission.
5. Helping parents for on line admission.
6. Promote research studies on RTE implementation.
7. Visiting schools with parents and insisting on to have RTE Cell at the time of admission.
8. Helping parents in follow up work.
9. Distributing pamphlet/patrika in vernacular language for the RTE Act awareness.
10. Meetings with parents at grassroot level.
11. Forming group for human rights awareness (networking).
12. Writing and sharing blogs/twitter/whats up/facebook/ mail etc for human rights awareness.
13. Organising conference/seminar and invite parents Govt. authority/media.
14. Prepare seminar report and send to policy-makers with recommendations.

At state level

- Each State should prepare a set of model rules for implementation of the RTE.
- The states must take steps to employ more qualified teachers and not to rely on para teachers to provide quality education.
- The govt. should ensure that all government schools are well equipped to take in students, so that they are not left with the sole choice of going to private school.
- School management committees should spread awareness about the Act at the community level, in panchayat.
- School management committees should be provided necessary financial and other support by the state to go about their duties.

- PPP model at primary level should be avoided at all costs so that there is no commercialization of education.
- There is a conflict between the child labour law and RTE Act, though both deal with related issues and promote the overall development of children. It is important to bring them in step, to avoid any confusion.
- To implement the RTE Act, effectively, the HRD Ministry, Panchayati Raj Ministry, Women and Child Development Ministry, Labour Ministry and Rural Development Ministry have to work in coordination. There should be an umbrella body that integrates all these bodies/agencies together to work towards a common goal and be accountable.
- The Govt. should make efforts to become self- sufficient by using education cess and other taxes to effectively implement RTE Act and to stop the tendency of dependency on private/foreign sector.

Conclusion

Thus, effective implementation of RTE Act 2009 is an important essential task. It needs collaborative and cooperative efforts by all i.e. Central Government, State Governments, statutory bodies, school managements, teachers, parents and students also. It seems difficult like Swacchata Abhiyan but quite possible up to great extent.

REFERENCES

International Covenant of Economic, *Social and Cultural Righ*ts 1966.

Mehta P.L. and Poonga Rakhee .(1997). Free and Compulsory Edu*cation, New Delhi: Deep and* Deep Publications.

Narayan V. and Reddy Karan (1979). Man, Education and Values, New Delhi, B.R. Publication.

RTE with special focus on corporal punishment-Reading material, NUEPA, New Delhi, October, 2014.

Universal Declaration of Human Rights, 1948.

6

Challenges of Decentralisation: An Approach for Realizing Children's Educational Rights from the Roots to Top

Asmi Siddiqui

In 21st century, on one hand, whole world is on the path of inclusive growth and sustainable development, on the other hand, human rights are guaranteed by all national and international laws in order to protect and promote individual rights and freedom. Genesis and presence of human right in society are the result of the efforts of those people who gave lot of sacrifices and pain for getting the rights for those people who were facing the discrimination of the society in the past. The word "right" is very easy to say but the implication of the right is very difficult like genesis of the term "right" in the history. In the normal discourse, the term human right means the rights of human but practically areas of human right are so wide and beyond the literary meaning of the term right. In this world, wherever human beings exist there will be a demand of rights to remove the disparities which are created by the people. While looking at the historical emergence of rights, we see that rights emerged because of unjust behaviour of certain sections of society with some underprivileged people. Human rights were declared in UDHR after the Second World War for making the people equal in all the aspects of life like Education, Employment, Health, Race, Freedom etc. However, emergence of human right is deeply rooted in some historical events like

American Revolution (Bill of Rights, 1791), French Revolution (1789), abolition of slavery in America (1865). The emergence of rights have evolved due to bitter and cruel experiences of the certain sections of the societies those were oppressed for centuries and the demands raised by them for the equality to lead a life with dignity and peace. A right is the weapon to make a person equal among unequals.

In Indian context, presently rights are associated with all articles of the Constitution of India which are mentioned in the Part 3 of the Constitution under article 12 to article 30 which give details of rights as right of liberty, right of freedom, right of education, right to employment, right of minorities etc. These constitutional articles which are covering certain rights are not the wholesome areas of rights for human. In reality, we will see the rights everywhere in all discourses of life. Here a question arises whether placing the right under the constitution is sufficient for the human to avail his/her right? Our constitution makers gave the provision of constitutional remedies under article 32 because they knew that there might be a violation of rights. Under the Constitution of India judiciary has been authorised to protect the fundamental rights of a man, right to education is one of them as defined under Article 21-A. Right to Education (RTE) is a milestone in the direction of assuring universal primary education. RTE in India belongs to all children of the country here the critical problem is that right to education is made for the children who are dependent upon their parents. The demand of right to education cannot be raised from the children that is why RTE will be successful only from the collective effort from the side of parents, local community, teachers, government administration and policymakers.

All the provisions are mentioned in the constitution but maximum population of India is illiterate and unaware for the children's right. Here a need emerges that parents should be well aware for the rights of children in respect of free education, free food, free dress, scholarship and monitoring the school functioning. For this purpose under RTE decentralisation approach adopted for giving the rights of education to each child of India. That is a good effort from the side of government but the implication and implementation of right is difficult as the genesis of Right to Education (RTE).

RTE is mentioned under the constitution of India in Article 45 and Article 21-A in that way: The Constitution (Eighty-sixth Amendment) Act, 2002 substituted Article 45 making provision for early childhood care and education to children below the age of six years in place of provision for free and compulsory education until they completed the age of fourteen years.[1] The Constitution (86th Amendment) Act, 2002 has added a new Article 21(A) after Article 21 and has made education for all children of the age of 6 to 14 a fundamental right. It provides "the state shall provide free and compulsory education to all children of the age of 6 to 14 years in such manner as the state may, by law, determine."[2]

That is the constitutional provision for the RTE act that came in 2009. Providing primary education on free basis is not a new thought for India, in fact, it came during colonial period. India being larger in population found difficult to give constitutional form for primary education. RTE provisions that are placed under the constitution came after the tremendous effort from our social reformers. Under the RTE the free education could be possible through Sarva Shiksha Abhiyan that is the main programme to give free and compulsory education. That dream was seen by Gopal Krishna Gokhale in Imperial legislative assembly but it could be realized in 2002 by giving rights to poor and underprivileged children of our country. Right of children to free and compulsory education (RTE) act, 2009 comes into force today. It is important to mention the name of our former Education Minister Maulana Abul Kalam Azad who desired that primary education should be provided on free basis in India so that everyone could get free education. After the independence when the framers of the Constitution were gathered in the constituent assembly to debate and discuss the provision of free and compulsory education justifiable, they first placed it under the Fundamental Rights and later placed it to Directive Principles of the state policy under Article 45.

Decentralized Approach and Legal Framework of Right to Education (RTE)

Adopting decentralisation under RTE to provide free education is not a new concept. It came during colonial period when Lord Mayo introduced financial decentralization in 1870s till then decentralized approach was adopted in India. Later decentralized approach was adopted in all Indian policies and programmes whether it was Mahatma Gandhi NREGA (MNREGA), Swarna Jayanti Gram Swarozgar Yojna (SJGSY), Nirmal Bharat Programme etc. In India, Right to Education traces back up to two centuries ago as clause 43 of the charter act, 1813 made education a state responsibility. Since then education came under the responsibility of state. In India education is laid down under the concurrent list that is the responsibility of both Centre and State. That is good approach that both Centre and State are key performers in the policy making and implementing RTE Act. A quotation is important to mention here that American President Woodrow Wilson wrote in his article 'Science of Administration' that "It is getting harder to run a Constitution than to write one".[3] That phrase is also applied in Right to Education (RTE) because India has made education a child right but giving place of a right under the constitution is different than giving the right to all children in reality. In that way to fulfill the child right, decentralisation approach adopted by the government of India to provide free and compulsory education as a child right is a good approach. It is a method in which the central authority invests certain powers to the local authorities to become autonomous in their fields. Decentralized primary educational planning starts from planning and monitoring from the *Gram Sabha* or *Ward* and it reaches to the higher level from ground. Implementation of RTE has adopted decentralised approach in which it is running from Central government, State government and local government. Presently, education comes under concurrent list means educational responsibilities will be fulfilled by both Central and State governments. Under the RTE it is said that state government is empowered to implement the RTE as per the need of the state. That process looks at the local government which is the last unit of government to implement

RTE through Gram Sabha. Local authorities are included under the RTE act to achieve the objectives that are mentioned under the RTE through decentralisation in that way: Local authority is defined under Section 2(h) as follows: "local authority" means a Municipal Corporation or Municipal Council or Zila Parishad or Nagar Panchayat or Panchayat, by whatever name called, and includes such other authority or body having administrative control over the school or empowered by or under any law for the time being in force to function as a local authority in any city, town or village."[4] The 73rd and 74th Amendments of the Constitution provide decentralization of education through *Panchayati Raj Institutions*/Municipal Corporation/Municipal Council. For community participation School Management Committee (SMC) introduced and duty of decentralized planning and monitoring have been laid down on the SMC. Earlier there was set up of Village Education Committee (VEC) and Ward Education Committee (WEC) but now all the task of these committees are performed by School Management Committee (SMC). Primary and Upper Primary schools organize a meeting in every month where problems are raised related to schools and children. Decentralised approach adopted to give the right to children for free education but it is not really effortless to plan from root level that roots are *Gram Sabha* and Ward of cities. Then for this purpose RTE laid down concept of community participation that is a support and backbone of government to run primary education with the help of nearby people. That could be possible from School Management Committee (SMC).

Involvement of Primary Education with Panchayati Raj Institutions

The Constitution of India (Article 243 G, 73rd Amendment Act) mandates the Gram Panchayat to prepare plans for economic development and social justice. Besides 73rd Amendment, 93rd Amendment bill also emphasizes the sharing of education related responsibility among various levels of government.[5] Gram Panchayats have been assigned to deal with primary education and dealing with that responsibility becomes a constitutional obligation for Panchayats. Panchayats and community will be directly involved through Gram Pradhan and they need not to go to higher authorities for conveying their ideas, needs and aspirations for education. The direct involvement of panchayats in primary education will make the education system more accountable and transparent as Panchayats are in closer proximity with community and they are answerable to the community through the Gram Sabha.

Legal Functions of SMC under the Uttar Pradesh RTE Rules, 2011

There is a procedure to set up a school management committee consisting of the elected representatives of the local authority, parents, or guardians children's admitted to, in these schools. It is provided that under the RTE that at least 3/4 of the members of that committee shall be parents and guardians. It is further provided in the act that 50% members of that committee shall be women.[6] All SMC members are part of programme to evaluate the working of schools in their neighbourhood schools. These people will be involved in decentralized planning to make plans for the schools in School Development Plan or *Shala Vikas Yojna*.

Functions of the school management committee are monitoring the working of the school, preparing and recommending school development plan, monitoring the utilisation of the grants received from appropriate government or local authority or any other source and perform such other functions as may be prescribed by the Act. It is also stated in the Act that school shall develop a School Development Plan/Shala Vikas Yojna under section 21. In the RTE act, all duties have been well described regarding qualification for appointments and norms, terms and conditions of the service of teachers, duties of teachers and redressal of grievances and pupil teachers ratio. It is clearly mentioned under the act that no teacher shall involve in non educational purposes and private tuitions. Teachers are provided to deal with only teaching task.[7]

Challenges before the RTE on Ground Level for Community Participation

All the provisions are mentioned under the constitution regarding community participation for grassroot planning. It is said that SMC will conduct meeting every month and all the members of the committee to take part in the meeting that is essential to check the reality of the implementation at the ground level. For this purpose when an empirical research was conducted in the Bareilly district of Uttar Pradesh, a sample was selected in which two blocks were taken from rural and urban block. Two blocks selected as Nagar Kshetra and Bithiri Chainpur for sample. Before analyzing results of study, it was necessary to know the geographical and economic features of sample Bareilly. Geographically, Bareilly is located in the western Uttar Pradesh. Economic data shows that Bareilly is hub of Bamboo work that's why it is called Baans-Bareilly, it is also recognized with the worldwide for Zari work, Manjhaa work etc. Bareilly has been received title of magnet city because citizens of neighbour cities are migrating to Bareilly due to opportunities of labour work and employment. Under the administrative structure, it was found that Department of Education is responsible for implementing RTE in the district. Implementation of Right to Education (RTE) in Bareilly is facing lot of problems due to long channels and mal-administration. There are number of reasons due to which RTE is affected. There is poor implementation of education right because of lack of education, awareness, non effective community participation at the grassroot level. All policies are constructed in the secretariat but it has to be implemented in the cities and villages of India. Then it becomes necessary to involve local people for achieving the right to education.

Despite various attractive provisions RTE is badly affected in implementation. It is essential to know the barriers, challenges, obstacles and problems related to planning from the roots. Legal framework of right to education is very good but decentralized approach is affected due to multiple channels, mal-administration, lack of awareness, poor supervision and from the lack of responsibility among teachers. In the survey, it is found that girls share 50% enrolment in total enrolment in primary schools of Bareilly that has motivating result. BSA office data showed that Bareilly has 50:50 enrolments of girls and boys. In total enrolment of children, minorities are more enrolled in urban schools as compared to the rural primary schools.

When survey was conducted in rural and urban primary schools it was found that all the rural and urban primary schools have constituted School Management Committee (SMC) in its schools. In all sample schools of urban area a committee was set up by the administration and school teachers. All committees were set up before 2009. The problem is not related to establishment of these committees but the actual contribution of these committees really matters. Nirdeshika is an information booklet which is given by the government for the school teachers to know about SMC and its role in schools. 4 out of 5 urban schools did not receive *Nirdeshika* by the administration. Among the five rural primary schools, 1 school got nirdeshika while other 4 schools did not receive nirdeshika. That is the duty of the Department of Education to circulate the Nirdeshika to all schools because when teachers receive that booklet then they would be able to know about the SMC and community participation. There is a major backdrop of the implementation of the policy that teachers and parents must be well aware about school management committee (SMC). That can be possible only when school receives *Nirdeshika*. From that booklet, parents and teachers will get to know about the purpose, importance and responsibilities of school management committee (SMC). In the survey, it was found there was hardly any knowledge about school development plan/Shala Vikas Yojna among teachers. That is one of the major critics for the RTE because of non participative and inactive role of administration. School teachers had listened to the concept of School Development Plan (Shala Vikaas Yojna) first time in questionnaire when questions were asked about school development plan. That is inefficiency and lack of awareness of the administration that they are unable to provide information details to school teachers to make School Development Plan. Major finding is that teachers don't know about School Development Plan in any of the schools. Here the reality of school development plan can be questioned. In all schools no school development plan was prepared. How it can be prepared if they do not know *Shala Vikas Yojna*. It is the duty of administration to inform them about *Shala Vikas Yojna* and to motivate them to develop school plan as per their need. Here the concept of community participation totally fails due to ineffective implementation of RTE. If administration distributes nirdeshika to school teachers, they will become aware about SMC's role in the preparation of the plan for their own schools as per their need of school and children. In sample schools in rural and urban blocks of Bareilly, various questions related to the Right to Education and teachers knowledge about RTE were raised, and then was found that teachers have little knowledge about the RTE norms.

Drop out is a serious issue of concern in all schools. Drop out training is given in most of the schools in summer session yearly but problem is that these trained children again did not come to school on regular basis. Infrastructure is one of the important reasons of poor quality of education because many classes are running in a single classroom. If teachers teach children in good and qualitative way they will not go to drop out stage.

Infrastructure quality is also associated with drop out and quality education. In this study, it is found that urban primary schools are worse in infrastructure as compared to the rural primary schools. Main reason is that in village area land can be easily allotted to schools which is not possible in urban area due to congestion of population and land. Non seriousness is also a reason that primary schools are suffering from. In rural Primary school, there are five rooms but two rooms are used by BRC office and one room is used for storeroom of BRC and only two rooms are used for teaching purposes. Despite the availability of rooms, students are not studying in classrooms due to lack of infrastructure. Another place should be provided to BRC for official purpose so that children can study in their own rooms. One Urban primary school is really in damaged condition and administration is not taking any action for its repair. That school is on rent and sharing of responsibility between local government and department of education is the main reason of conflict for repair work in school.

Among the total 10 schools teachers are not well aware with Right to Education 2009 while administration gave training to all teachers to make them aware with RTE but teachers responded that BRC, CRC and departmental trainings are not qualitatively good. Teachers in 4 schools out of 10 schools told that administrative officials demand bribe from the schools.

Administration is giving proper training to all SMC members including teachers and parents. Four members from each school were trained by CRC and BRC to give information about School Management Committee (SMC). Another issue was found that NPRC will help teachers for syllabus and curriculum but it is found that all NPRC's are not performing their teaching task which is assigned to them. They are just performing their official work. Right to Education is good in itself but it is lagging behind due to lack of unawareness. But the fact is that if parents will not know about their rights how can they monitor SMC. It is important that people, parents, teachers, administration should be well aware about education rights. In that way education of rights is important. Rights education and awareness are needed today among people to become equal among unequals.

REFERENCES

1. Basu, Dr Durga Das (2010). *Introduction to the constitution of India*. (20th Ed.) Nagpur: LexisNexis Butterworth Wadhwa. p. 153.
2. Pandey, J.N. (2003). *Constitutional Law of India* (40th Edition) Allahabad: Central Law Agency. p. 256.
3. Bhattacharya, Mohit. (2008). *New Horizons of Public Administration*. New Delhi: Jawahar Publishers and Distributors. p. 4.

4. Framework for Implementation, Based on the Right of Children Free and Compulsory Education Act, 2009, Ministry of HRD, 2011. p. 112.

5. Laxmikant, M. (2006). *Public Administration*. New Delhi: Tata McGraw Hill Publishing Company Limited. p. 531.

6. The Uttar Pradesh Right of Children to Free and Compulsory Education Rules, 2011.

7. Gazette of Government of India, The Right of Children to Free and Compulsory Education Act., 2009, p. 7.

7

Human Rights Education: Developing Ethical Quotient

Usha Pathak

The goal of a human rights-based approach to education is simple: to assure every child a quality education that respects and promotes her or his right to dignity and optimum development.

The right to education is high on the agenda of the international community. It is affirmed in numerous human rights treaties and recognized by governments as pivotal in the pursuit of development and social transformation. This recognition is exemplified in the international goals, strategies and targets that have been set during the past 20 years. The Education for All goals were established at Jomtien (Thailand) in 1990 and reaffirmed at the 2000 World Education Forum in Dakar (Senegal).

However, the progress made to date is far from adequate. In many regions, girls lag far behind. In other regions, there is a growing problem of underachievement by boys. Poverty is a key factor impeding enrolment, primary and secondary completion, and learning outcomes, and children from ethnic minority and indigenous communities consistently under access. The evidence indicates that, on current trajectories, the international targets for access will not be met.

Many international agencies have, therefore, increasingly turned to a human rights-based approach. As early as 1997, as part of the United Nations Programme for Reform, the UN Secretary-General called on all entities of the UN system to bring human rights into the mainstream of their activities and programmes. The outcome was the UN Statement of Common Understanding, which integrates international human rights into plans, strategies and policies associated with development programmes. The rights-based approach focuses on the inalienable human rights of each individual, as expressed in UN instruments, and on governments' obligation to fulfil, respect and protect those internationally defined human rights. In doing so, it aims to support and empower individuals and communities to claim their rights. In addition, a distinctive feature of this approach is that it requires an equal commitment to both process and outcomes.

Human Rights Education History

The emphasis on Human Rights Education began in 1995 with the beginning of the UN Decade for Human Rights Education, though previously addressed in 1953 with the UNESCO Associated Schools Program, which served as an "initial attempt to teach human rights in formal school settings". The first formal request for the need to educate students about human rights came about in UNESCO's 1974 article Recommendation concerning Education for International Understanding, Cooperation and Peace, and Education Relating to Human Rights and Fundamental Freedoms. The participants of the International Congress on the Teaching of Human Rights eventually met in 1978 to form a specific definition of what would be required application of the education in formal curricula. The aims at which the Congress agreed upon including the encouragement of tolerant attitudes with focus on respect, providing knowledge of human rights in the context of national and international dimensions as well as their implementations, and finally developing awareness of human rights translating into reality whether social or political on national and international levels.

Human Rights Education became an official central concern internationally after the World Conference on Human Rights in 1993. This conference brought the issue of educating formally to the top of many countries' priority lists and was brought to the attention of the United Nations. It was two years later that the United Nations approved the Decade for Human Rights Education, which reformed the aims of application once again.

Since, the development of the UN Decade, the incorporation of human rights education into formal school curricula has been developed and diversified with the assistance of nongovernmental organizations, intergovernmental organizations, and individuals dedicated to spreading the topic through formal education.

Today the most influential document used to determine what qualifies as human rights and how to implement these ideas and rights into everyday life is the Universal Declaration. This declaration was adopted by the General Assembly in 1948, making December 10 annual Human Rights Day ever since. To this day the 30 article compilation is seen as "a common standard of achievement for all peoples and all nations".

Why Human Rights Education?

Human rights are highly inspirational and also highly practical, embodying the hopes and ideals of most human beings and also empowering people to achieve them. Human rights education shares those inspirational and practical aspects. It sets standards but also produces change. Effective human rights education can—

- Produce changes in values and attitudes
- Produce changes in behaviour
- Produce empowerment for social justice
- Develop attitudes of solidarity across issues, communities, and nations
- Develop knowledge and analytical skills
- Encourage participatory education.

Human Rights Education (HRE): Indian Scenario

Article 51 A(l) of Indian Constitution 1950, imposes a duty on all citizens to develop scientific temper, humanism and the spirit of inquiry and reform. The effective discharge of this duty will require HRE to give people enhanced awareness and greater openness. Right to education has also been incorporated. The Constitution mandates the state to direct its policy towards securing that children are given opportunities and facilities to develop in a healthy manner and in conditions of freedom and dignity and that childhood and youth are protected against exploitation and against moral and material abandonment. HRE for the children as well as the other people is indispensable to the full realization of the responsibility under this constitutional directive. Indian state has an obligation to foster respect for international law and treaty obligations as laid down in Article 51 of the Constitution. India is a signatory to UDHR and has ratified Civil and Political Rights Convention, Economic, Social and Cultural Rights Convention, CEDAW CRC, etc. HRE is inescapable and a legal obligation. HRE can foster a spirit of respect for others and high citizenship qualities. Citizenship in a democracy involves many intellectual, social and moral qualities a democratic citizen should have the under standing and an intellectual integrity to sift truth from falsehood, facts from propaganda and to reject the dangerous appeal of fanaticism and prejudice should neither reject the old because it is old nor accept the new because it is new, but dispassionately examine both and courageously reject what arrests the forces of justice and progress.

HRE is important because it can prevent violation of human rights, promote assertion of human rights. Human rights is an essential part of social studies curriculum. The National System of Education envisages a common educational structure. The 10+2+3 structure has now been accepted in all parts of the country. Regarding the further break-up of the first 10 years, efforts will be made to move towards an elementary system comprising five years of primary education and three years of upper primary, followed by two years of High School. Higher Education follows in graduate, postgraduate and doctoral degree programmes in various subjects including management, professions and technology. The National Policy on Education underlines the importance of value education. The growing concern over the erosion of essential values and an increasing cynicism in society has brought to focus the need for readjustments in the curriculum in order to make education a forceful tool for the cultivation of social and moral values.

'Human Rights' is not treated as a separate subject in the curricula. NCERT has felt that all contemporary concerns and issues cannot be included in the curriculum as separate subjects of study. It has called upon incorporation of certain emerging concerns including human rights in the course content. This is in line with the UNESCO suggestion. Human rights education cannot be reduced to the simple introduction of human rights content in already overburdened curricula. It brings about a profound reform of education, which touches upon curriculum in—service and pre-service training, textbooks, methodology, classroom management and the organization of the education system atall levels. But it is disappointing to observe that the NCF 2005 has failed in identifying the content of the HRE in schools. University Grants Commission appointed Sikri Committee in 1980 to consider and report on the different ways and means for promoting HRE in India. The committee suggested inculcating values without marks weight-age in schools. At college levels it was felt that all disciplines should be including human rights topics at least which are directly relevant to their disciplines. Now HRE is part of many university programmes. Interestingly, certificate, diploma, postgraduate diploma and even masters programme in human rights are available today. Bar Council of India has made human rights a compulsory subject for professional law degree programme. Many universities offer human rights subject for post graduate programme in law.

Rights Based Approach to Education

Need-based development approaches to education have failed to achieve the Education for All goals. Because it is inclusive and provides a common language for partnership, a rights-based approach—although certainly not without tensions and challenges—has the potential to contribute to the attainment of the goals of governments, parents and children. Girls' right to education, for example, can be achieved more effectively if measures are also implemented to address their rights to freedom from discrimination, protection from exploitative labour, physical violence and sexual abuse, and access to an adequate standard of living. Equally, the right to education is instrumental in the realization of other rights. Research indicates, for example, that one additional year of schooling for 1,000 women helps prevent two maternal deaths.

A rights-based approach can contribute significant added value:

- **It promotes social cohesion, integration and stability:** Human rights promote democracy and social progress. Even where children have access to school, a poor quality of education can contribute to dissatisfaction. A rights-based approach to education, which emphasises quality, can encourage the development of school environment in which children know their views are valued. It includes a focus on respect for families and the values of the society in which they are living. It can also promote understanding of other cultures and peoples, contributing to intercultural dialogue and respect for the richness of cultural and linguistic diversity, and the right to participate in cultural life. In this way, it can serve to strengthen social cohesion.
- **It builds respect for peace and non-violent conflict resolution:** A rights-based approach to education is founded on principles of peace and non-violent conflict resolution. In achieving this goal, schools and communities must create learning environment that eliminates all forms of physical, sexual or humiliating punishment by teachers and challenges all forms of bullying and aggression among students. In other words, they must promote and build a culture of non-violent conflict resolution. The lessons children learn from school-based experiences in this regard can have far-reaching consequences for the wider society.
- **It contributes to positive social transformation:** A rights-based approach to education that embodies human rights education empowers children and other stakeholders and represents a major building block in efforts to achieve social transformation towards rights-respecting societies and social justice.

- **It is more cost-effective and sustainable:** Treating children with dignity and respect—and building inclusive, participatory and accountable education system that responds directly to the expressed concerns of all stakeholders—will serve to improve educational outcomes. In too many schools, the failure to adapt to the needs of children, particularly working children, results in high levels of dropout and repeated grades. Children themselves cite violence and abuse, discriminatory attitudes, an irrelevant curriculum and poor teaching quality as major contributory factors in the inability to learn effectively and in subsequent dropout. In addition, health issues can diminish the ability of a child to commence and continue schooling, and for all children, especially girls, an inclusive education can reduce the risk of HIV infection. A rights-based approach is therefore not only cost-effective and economically beneficial but also more sustainable.
- **It produces better outcomes for economic development:** A rights-based approach to education can be entirely consistent with the broader agenda of governments to produce an economically viable workforce. Measures to promote universal access to education and overcome discrimination against girls, children with disabilities, working children, children in rural communities, and minority and indigenous children will serve to widen the economic base of society, thus strengthening a country's economic capability.
- **It builds capacity:** By focusing on capacity-building and empowerment, a rights-based approach to education harnesses and develops the capacities of governments to fulfil their obligations and of individuals to claim their rights and entitlements.

Human Rights Education Models

- Values and Awareness: The Values and Awareness Model focuses on transmitting "basic knowledge of human rights issues and to foster its integration into public values" based on its philosophical-historical approach. This model is what people commonly think of when human rights are concerned with the target audience being the general public with topics including global human rights and more culture based matters.

- Accountability: The Accountability Model is associated with the legal and political approach to human rights in which the learners which the model targets are already involved via professional roles. The model is incorporated by means of training and networking, covering topics such as court cases, codes of ethics, and how to deal with the media.
- Transformational: This model of education focuses on the psychological and sociological aspects of human rights. The topics towards which this model is effective are those including vulnerable populations and people with personal experiences effected by the topic, such as women and minorities. The model aims to empower the individual, such as those victims of abuse and trauma. The model is geared towards recognizing the abuse of human rights but is also committed to preventing these abuses.

Programme Planning, Design and Implementation

A rights-based approach to programming recognizes that the process of development is as important as the outcome. Indeed, the process largely determines the type of outcome resulting from development activities. The principles that inform a rights-based approach outlined below should be taken into consideration in the planning, design and implementation of programmes.

- Universality and inalienability
- Indivisibility
- Interdependence and interrelatedness
- Equality and non-discrimination
- Participation and Inclusion

- Empowerment
- Accountability and respect for the rule of law

Although, not all are new to development practice participation and accountability. For example, these are also characteristic of good programming—the added value of a rights-based approach is that such principles acquire moral and political force. This is important, given that the people who may benefit the most from the application of these principles, i.e., poor and marginalized groups, are not generally in a position to claim their rights.

Taking a rights-based approach to education will necessitate that:

- The programme engages with government in a constructive dialogue regarding its obligations, and how best it can fulfil these. This may require incentives and technical assistance, as well as capacity-building.
- Claims holders are involved in the assessment, decision-making and implementation of education provision.
- Evidence-based advocacy is used to increase the scale of impact through, for example, replication, legislative and policy change, and resource allocation.
- Special attention is paid to the most marginalized and discriminated against groups. This approach involves going beyond addressing poorer communities to identify the most vulnerable people among the poor, for example, children with disabilities, children in low castes, internally displaced persons and children living with HIV. It then develops programming specifically to reach them.
- All programme activities are explicitly linked to human rights standards. Such standards set minimum guarantees for poor and disadvantaged groups. They also help identify where problems exist and what capacities and functions are required to address them. In the programming process, human rights standards can help define a comprehensive but targeted scope

for development strategies that will yield more cost-effective results. They can also help to set results-based outcomes and outputs.

Monitoring and Evaluation

A rights-based approach to monitoring and evaluating education has implications, beyond those that would be addressed as good development practice, for both the process by which it is undertaken and the outcome, it seeks to measure. In terms of process, there is a need for greater transparency of information about education provision. In addition, children and their communities need to be actively engaged as partners and involved in design, analysis, sharing of information and documentation. Their involvement empowers them and improves the quality of the information. Such monitoring and evaluation frameworks will help capture both the qualitative and quantitative indicators in respect of realising the rights-based approach to education. In terms of outcome, monitoring and evaluation need to address:

- Changes in the lives of children to measure whether their education rights are better realized or no longer violated.
- Changes in legislation, policy, structures and practices and their impact on the realization of educational rights.
- Changes in relation to equity and non-discrimination in respect of access to education, the quality of that education and the experience of children within it. For example, have more marginalized children been reached and have discriminatory references in the curriculum been removed?
- Opportunities for participation and active citizenship of children as well as other stakeholders, in schools and in the wider development of education policy.
- Changes in civil society and community capacity to support the rights-based approach—for example, through advocacy for improved education, active

support for local schools, and ensuring the equal right of girls and boys.

Role of Teachers

The teachers relate to administrators, parents, community members, other staff and students. In relationship with students, teachers are clearly super ordinate. The recognition of the power of the teacher is the predominant feature of the relationship between the teacher and the student. The teacher plays the roles of diagnostician and prognostician of student behaviour, planner, initiator and supervisor of classroom learning activities, evaluator, model, counsellor and guide, disciplinarian, machine operator and clerk.

Even before we embark on HRE, the teachers should know the rights of children and respect them. As teachers, it is not just what we teach matters, but it is also what we do. Equality, the principle that is in the best interests of the child shall be the primary consideration in actions concerning children and respect for the views of the child are the general principles of the Convention on the Rights of a Child.

Children have right to leisure, play, recreational & cultural activities, apart from civil rights, liberties, right to health, right to family environment and educational right. While devising classroom activities, disciplining, and evaluating, the interests of the child shall be borne in mind. 'Student Welfare' shall be the beacon light guiding all actions.

Responsibilities of Teachers in HRE

- Bring to the notice of other teachers, the Principal, the text book writers and the concerned government authority any aberrations in textbooks. Wrong messages should have no room. The textbooks should be meticulously examined.
- Take initiatives to enrich the school library and personal collection with books and materials on human rights.
- Resolve not to violate human rights. Object to and take efforts to correct human rights violations in the school.

Lack of basic facilities like water and sanitation, denial of recess for students, excessive corporal punishments, in dignifying remarks, etc. shall not be there. Conditions of mutual respect shall prevail in the dealings with parents, other staff and community.

- Teachers should not merely follow the textbooks prescribed. Examination of school syllabus is neither adequate. Teachers are to be prepared to analyse the curricular framework and policy implications. Objectives laid down shall be understood and realized.
- Teachers shall give adequate importance to duty education as well. Indian society is duty based and HRE must aim at accepting responsibilities by following that for every right there is a responsibility. Duties under Indian Constitution and UDHR shall be emphasized.

Human Rights Education Organization

- Arab Institute for Human Rights
- African Centre on Democracy and Human Rights Studies
- African Commission on Human and People Rights
- African Commission on Human and People Rights
- Amnesty International
- The Asian Human Rights Commission
- The Australian Council for Human Rights
- The Chapel Hill and Carrboro Human Rights Centre
- Children's Defence Fund (CDF)
- Coalition for Human Rights Education (COHRE)
- United Nations Human Rights Council
- Human Rights Watch
- United Nations Education, Scientific and Cultural Organization (UNESCO)

REFERENCES

Geneva Conventions, 1949

Illustrations: UDHR 1948, Declaration on Elimination of all Forms of Discrimination Against Women 1967, Declaration onRights of a Child 1959, Vienna Declaration 1993, etc.

International Congress on Education for Human Rights and Democracy, Montreal, 1993 (UNESCO).

Teaching Human Rights, United Nations, New York, 1989 p. 5.

U.N. Charter, Article 1(3)

What is HRE? www.unesco.org

http://www.un.org/Overview/rights.html

http://www2.ohchr.org/english/law/pdf/vienna.pdf

http://portal.unesco.org/education/en/ev.php-

http://www.rightsedu.net/

8

Inclusive Education at Crossroads: Preparing Schools to Meet the Challenge

Chetna Thapa

"Neglected, marginalized are common in knowledge world. We are not the sources of problems. We are the resources that are needed to solve them. We are not expenses, we are investments. We are the children of the world and despite our different backgrounds we share a common reality. We are united in our struggle to make the world a better place for all."

Ms. Gabriela Arrieta—Opening address at the UN Special Session on Children, May 2002

It is now widely acknowledged that to achieve the goal of universal education in India and in order to fulfil provisions laid out in the Right of Children to Free and Compulsory Education (RTE) Act, 2009 (Ministry of Human Resource Development, 2009) the education of children with disabilities cannot be put on the back burner. Inclusion or the education of children with disabilities in regular classrooms must be adopted both as an ideology and as a practical solution to support the Education for All, and to bring about equity in education in India. In this context, this paper argues for individual initiative on part of schools to extend facilities for children with disabilities within their regular school settings. The paper further provides guidelines that schools can adopt to set up inclusive education practices.

Understanding Inclusive Education

Inclusive education means that schools should accommodate all children regardless of their physical, intellectual, social, emotional, linguistic or other conditions. This should include disabled and gifted children, street and working children, children from remote or nomadic populations, children from linguistic, ethnic or cultural minorities and children from other disadvantaged or marginalized areas or groups (UNESCO, 2003). Inclusive education is a pairing of philosophy and pedagogical practices that allow each student to feel respected, confident and safe so he or she can learn and develop to his or her full potential. It is based on a belonging, active participation in learning, a complete school experience, and positive interactions with peers and others in the school community. These values and beliefs will be shared by schools and communities. Inclusive education is put into practice within school communities that value diversity and nurture the well-being and quality of learning of each of their members. Inclusive education is carried out through a range of public and community programmes and services available to all students.

The goal of an inclusive education system is to provide all students with the most appropriate learning environments and opportunities for them to best achieve their potential.

Policy Support for Inclusive Education

As mentioned earlier, inclusive education has been embraced in policy and in principle as the way forward by all major establishments related to elementary education in India in general and disability in particular in the last two decades. Originating from the Salamanca World Conference on Special Needs Education (UNESCO, 1994), which Ainscow and Cesar (2006) referred to as "the most significant international document that has ever appeared in the field of special education" (p. 231), inclusive education received widespread recognition across the world. In India, schemes such as the Integrated Education for Disabled Children, IEDC (1974) launched by the Government of India and the Project Integrated Education of Disabled Children, PIEDC, launched during the Sixth Five-Year Plan (1985-89), had laid the foundation for inclusive education to be adopted at least in principle. The IEDC scheme was replaced by the Inclusive Education of the Disabled at Secondary Stage (IEDSS) in 2008 (NUEPA, 2009). The District Primary Education Programme (DPEP) adopted the inclusive education philosophy in 1997 (Sanjeev and Kumar, 2007). The Persons with Disability Act (Equal Opportunities, Protection of Rights and Full Participation) 1995 emphatically stated the need for equal opportunities for persons with disability and directed state and local authorities to take appropriate action towards meeting the goal. The Rights of Persons with Disability Bill, 2012, yet to be tabled in the Parliament spells out the goals of inclusive education with a clear sense of direction. The Bill directs educational institutions to provide inclusive education to children with disability with respect to admission, identification, infrastructure, teacher training, social and academic development, educational aids, curriculum and examination reforms (Ministry of Social Justice and Empowerment, 2011). Policy support for inclusion gained impetus with the launch of programmes like the Sarva Shiksha Abhiyan (SSA) during the Tenth Plan (2001) and the Right to Education Act, 2009. Undoubtedly, an important milestone in India's struggle to achieve the elusive Education for All goals, the Act provided the much needed patronage for education of children with special needs as well. It is clear that the goals set out for achievement of universal education in India go hand in hand with the principles of inclusion. Leaving behind children with disability in this race would therefore be both counterproductive and frivolous. The National Curriculum Framework (NCF), 1995 (National Council of Educational Research and Training, 2005) pointed to reforms in this very direction. However, even though support for inclusive education in India looks promising in policy, it cannot be overemphasized that the incongruity between policy and practice remains an unfathomable challenge. The mere existence of ambitious goals in policy has not ensured their expression so as to reach anywhere near the desired results.

This paper attempts to build a case for individual effort on part of schools to provide inclusive education facilities within their regular settings. As one looks towards achieving the goal of universal education for all children in the elementary years, it is up to schools to take the lead and brace themselves for the challenge. As the RTE mandates involvement of both private and public players in the process, no school can afford to escape responsibility. Further, it must be emphasized that an inclusive education programme in a school cannot exist as an appendage. It requires holistic involvement and participation of school personnel at all levels of administration and academic decision-making. As long as the provisions benefit the child and are cognizant of the child's developmental, social and emotional needs, different models of inclusion can be experimented with. In this context, guidelines for implementing programmes for children with disabilities in regular school settings are presented in the following sections.

The following premises form the basis for the guidelines:

1. Schools can implement inclusive education programmes at their own initiative.
2. Schools must be fully convinced and committed to the objectives of inclusive education.

   Consent and wholehearted support of the school management and personnel is pertinent to the success of the initiative.
3. The central recipient of the services is the child. Hence, creating an optimum environment to optimize the benefits to the child should be the primary objective of the programme.
4. The nature of the programme should be flexible and in the form of a continuum such that it can be adapted to suit each individual child's academic and social needs.
5. Schools must be cognizant of their strengths and weaknesses in order to adapt the guidelines based on their institutional nature and characteristics.

The following endeavors on part of the school may help:

(a) The administration must be aware of inherent factors within the school that may hamper the success of the programme. Shortage of teaching staff, possibility of resistance from parents, acute shortage of funds, poor administrative control and lack of infrastructure in the school, are likely to pose impediments in setting up of the programme. It is important to rule out these factors or to resolve these issues at the outset.

(b) Support of all teaching and administrative staff is desirable for effective programme implementation. Initially, a questionnaire may be circulated among teachers (with the option of anonymity) to gauge their attitude towards inclusion and disability in general.

(c) **Preparing the Teachers:** Small group meetings with teachers may be held where the administrator presents the programme in a formal manner. Free expression of ideas and apprehensions should be permitted during such meetings to allow teachers to clarify their doubts and seek appropriate answers.

(d) It is desirable that at least a few regular teachers of the school undergo specialized training to work with children with special needs. Short-term and ongoing in-service training programmes for teachers organized by governmental agencies such as the National Council for Teacher Education (NCTE) or a local NGO may prove useful in this regard. Gradually, these skills must be imparted to all the teachers of the school.

(e) **Preparing the Children:** Just as preparation of teachers is essential for the success of the programme, all the children of the school must be sensitized about the purpose of the programme and the children attending it. It is critical that children are presented with facts and that the sensitization process is not a onetime affair. Constant reinforcement is necessary for children to truly appreciate and respect diverse needs of children with different abilities. Storytelling, role plays, informal discussions in class and sharing of experiences by children attending the programme are some steps that the school may consider to undertake. Teachers must present information to the children in a factual manner and the programme should be projected as integral to the school.

(f) **Preparing the Parents:** Parents of all the children in the school must undergo orientation and sensitization to ensure their full cooperation. Interaction with experts, meeting with administrative heads and teachers should be used to educate parents about the need for such a programme. It should be highlighted during these interactions that the presence of children with special needs in the classroom is likely to improve the teaching-learning experience of all the children and help in their holistic growth and development. Wholehearted participation of parents is imperative for the success of any such initiative.

(g) **Infrastructure:** Based on the type of disabilities the school is likely to admit, the school must make some basic infrastructural changes. Building of ramps, railings, disability friendly toilets, and magnified sign boards may be some of these. However, if only children with learning disability are likely to be admitted in the beginning, these preparations may not be necessary. Providing facilities for physiotherapy, occupational therapy and speech therapy are desirable within the school setting but need not be considered as preconditions to setting up the programme. It may be a good idea to have a space designated within the school premises to carry out the functions of the programme during the initial phases. This room may be labeled as the Resource Room which all the children of the school could identify as a place where some of the children spend some of their school time learning and doing activities. Setting up the room in an interesting and creative manner is likely to generate positivity and not invite ridicule or resentment from the children. In fact, it may be a good idea to encourage all the children to walk into the room and explore it in order to alleviate their curiosity and to spend some time doing interesting activities. The room should be centrally located and not deliberately hidden from the main buildings and activities of the school. It may be noted that the room need not be set up opulently. A simple, basic and child friendly setting is likely to prove more accessible and useful. The room may also be used by teachers to store teaching aids, brainstorm ideas, learn new teaching techniques and exchange student information.

The Implementation Process

As the school prepares itself for the setting up procedures of admission and screening must be laid out. Although, it is eventually desired that all children, irrespective of the nature of their learning need and disability be part of the regular school system, it is important to be adequately prepared for the challenge. If the resources and facilities in the school do not permit such a scenario to begin with, it is sensible to be restrictive and admit only those children that the school is well-prepared to work within the initial stages. For instance, if infrastructure support or a trained teacher to help a visually impaired child is not available in a school, the child is unlikely to gain from such inclusion. Intervention process, curricular adaptations and teaching strategies require careful planning and must be worked out in detail. Intervention procedures and organizational aspects of the programme must be worked out through a coordinated effort among the regular teachers, resource room teachers, administrative staff and parents. Students should be allocated to attend classes based on their ability, performance level, special learning needs as well as competence of teachers in handling the learning needs. Issues of grouping, frequency of interaction with the special educators, areas which require specialized help, need for psychological counselling etc. are some matters that must be resolved through consultation with all the stakeholders.

Curriculum Adaptation and Teaching Strategies

Adapting curriculum to suit the individual need of each child is central to the ideology of an inclusive education programme. It is important here to reiterate the 'whole school approach' and involvement of all concerned personnel in the process. Undoubtedly, making curriculum adaptations is a huge challenge considering the constraints imposed by large classroom sizes examination driven teaching practices, poor teacher training, among other systemic rigidities that are a part of our school system. Hence, it is recommended that adaptations to the curriculum are made in a phased manner and with the support of all personnel concerned. Apart from imparting academic concepts, children may be given tips on organizing their work, following complex instructions by breaking them down, developing regular work habits, simplifying text, note-taking, drawing conceptual maps and improving oral communication skills. Including extra-curricular activities as an integral component of the curriculum for the children with special needs must be emphasized. This would go a long way in boosting their self-confidence, learning new skills, exploring creative abilities and most importantly, in enabling their social and emotional adjustment. When all the children of the school participate in school activities equally in a non-threatening environment, inclusion would truly happen.

Teaching methods adopted to work with children in the classroom must complement curriculum adaptations. Goal directed, individualized strategies using methods like preparing the Individualized Education Plan (IEP) are recommended. Special attention may be paid to pace of learning and the level of performance of each child in class. In general, it would be beneficial for all the children in class if strategies like problem solving, experimentation, questioning, and concentrating on areas of difficulty are encouraged more than rote learning. Short breaks to retain attention span, peer teaching, co-teaching with Resource Room teachers, and using creative and interactive teaching aids are likely to support curriculum adaptations.

Undoubtedly, challenges for classroom teachers are immense if they have children with diverse learning needs in the classroom. Support from the administration, parents and opportunities to acquire new learning techniques through training can raise their morale and help teachers take on the challenge. The key to success also lays in internalizing the ideals of inclusion and recognizing the fact that innovative teaching practice and individualized attention benefit all children and make the teaching learning process more effective and satisfying.

Evaluation

Just as curriculum adaptations and teaching strategies need to be adapted to suit learning needs of each child in the classroom, methods of evaluating their performance must undergo modifications too. Some relevant points to keep in mind in this regard are:

(a) Children with special needs in the classroom should be assessed on the individual abilities and progress. Unfair comparisons with other children should be avoided.

(b) Criterion-referenced testing methods may be adopted.

(c) Evaluation should be conducted on a regular basis using several criteria instead of just one. Substituting written exercises with oral assessment, discounting spelling errors, providing a scribe, giving extra time during examinations, reducing syllabi, exemption from studying some topics or including non-academic activities as criteria for assessment could be options that may prove useful based on each child's ability and learning need.

Role Allocation and Interaction Among Stakeholders

Effective coordination and cooperation among key personnel and all the stakeholders are essential for the programme to run efficiently. Some general guidelines may be followed in this regard:

1. Role allocation must be based on the personnel's expertise and willingness to be involved in the programme.
2. Clear delegation of roles is desirable to ensure smooth functioning of the programme.
3. Team work over delegation of assignment based on hierarchy should be encouraged.

4. A formal and effective means of communication, electronic and/or oral must be established to enable documentation and exchange of ideas among the personnel.
5. Continuous feedback and opportunities to express concerns and apprehensions must be provided to motivate personnel and address attitudinal issues.
6. Scheduling regular meetings among administrative staff, regular and resource teachers and with parents is of critical importance. Discussion of progress of each child, issues related to their social and emotional adjustment, enhancing teaching strategies and garnering support from parents and the peer group should be on the agenda.
7. **Parent Support:** Parents can play a key role in ensuring success of the programme. The parent-teacher dyad can lend strong support and impetus to the programme because they share similar goals and concerns. Establishing clear channels of communication, seeking parent support for identification of the problem, preparation of the intervention plan and keeping them abreast with the teaching methods and progress of their child on a regular basis could be a few initiatives in this direction.
8. **Peer Support:** Just as parents can lend support to the programme, the peer group too should form an integral component of the implementation process. In an inclusive setting peer support can be sought in different ways. For instance, peers can play an important role in ensuring that children with special needs are not socially and academically isolated. Peer tutoring, cooperative learning, mentoring, reciprocal teaching in the classroom, participation in extra-curricular activities together and grouping of mixed-ability children for outdoor activities and during free hours are some such measures. Teachers may have to pay extra attention to ensure that there are no incidents of ridicule or discrimination against any of the children by the peer group.

Programme Evaluation

All aspects of the programme must be evaluated on a regular basis. Some parameters for evaluation of the programme could be: monitoring the intake of children, assessment and identification procedures, attitude of teachers, parents and peers, degree of participation of all personnel, adequacy and availability of resources, reviewing training inputs required for curriculum adaptation and teaching methods, performance of children and impact of the programme on all the children and the institution in general. It must be asserted that even if at the time of initiation, the programme does not fulfil all criteria for being truly inclusive, continuous effort must be made to strive toward such a goal.

Conclusion

The above guidelines summarize a set of recommendations that schools can adopt to implement inclusive education programmes for children with special needs within their regular set up. It is pertinent that schools that initiate such programmes assess their strengths and weaknesses at the outset and ensure adequate cooperation from the school management as well as the administrative and teaching staff. It is important to state here that an inclusive education programme does not require resource overload or elaborate preparations. With policy support, opportunities for training of teachers and cooperation from parents and the peer group, inclusive practices can be effectively adopted by any school.

REFERENCES

Ainscow, M. and Cesar, M. (2006). Inclusive education ten years after Salamance: Setting the agenda. *European Journal of Psychology of Education*, XXI, 3, pp. 231-38.

Hodkinson, A. and Devarakonda, C. (2009). Conceptions of inclusion and inclusive education: A critical examination of the perspectives and practices of teachers in India. *Research in Education*, 82, pp. 85-99.

Joshi, P. (2010). Developing a vision for inclusive education: A case-study. In N. Sharma (Ed.), *The Social Ecology of Disability* (Technical series 3, Lady Irwin College, pp. 77-85). New Delhi.

India: Academic Excellence. Ministry of Human Resource Development, Government of India (2009). Right of children to free and compulsory education (RTE) act, 2009. Retrieved from http://mhrd.gov.in/rte Ministry of Social Justice and Empowerment (2011). The draft rights of persons with disability bill 2012, Retrieved from http://socialjustice.nic.in/pwd2011.php

National Council of Educational Research and Training (2005). The national curriculum framework. Retrieved from http://www.ncert.nic.in/rightside/links/pdf/framework/english/nf2005.pdf

Sharma, N. and Sen, Sharma, R. (2012). Children with disabilities and supportive school ecologies. In M. Ungar (Ed.), *The Social Ecology of Resilience: A handbook of theory and practice.* doi: 10.1007/978-1-4614-0586-3_22. New York: Springer.

9

Dynamics in Development Discourses: Possibility and Role of Human Rights Education

Rajlakshmi Datta

The Background

The developmental discourses the world over witnessed a paradigm shift from 'growth centric development' to more 'human centric development'. Although history has witnessed for many decades a customary focus on GDP as a measure of a country's well-being, yet as time passed by, there has been a growing concern in developing broad measures of economic well-being. Some endeavors at the national and international level have been 'beyond GDP programme' developed by the European Union, the Better Lives Compendium of Indicators developed by the OECD, as well as many alternative measures of well-being. The growing consensus is that traditional economic measures need to be supplemented by other measures founded in a more holistic view of human progress. The debate on the relationship between economic growth and human development, which dominated the political scene for decades, was clarified by scholars working with the UN Development Programme (UNDP). In 1990 the agency began to promote a new vision of human development in its first Human Development Report (UNDP, 1990). The last few years of UNDP analysis have contributed to an improved understanding of the relationship between economic growth and human development, concluding that development is not exclusively tied either to economic growth or human development, but rather to both. Interestingly the 2000 Human Development Report associated human development with human rights.

It is evident that the original focus of human development approaches was primarily on social and economic development as an outcome of development efforts. These approaches were less concerned with the quality of the course by which outcomes were achieved. Human Rights Approaches, on the other hand, place primary stress on an elaborate web of duties and obligations, and focus primarily on accountability and process. The Human Development Report 2000 acknowledges: "Although human development thinking has always insisted on the importance of the process of development, many of the tools developed by the human development approach measure the outcomes of social arrangements in a way that is not sensitive to how these outcomes were brought about" (UNDP, 2000). Human Rights Approaches go beyond Human Development Approaches by recognising that to achieve human development outcomes, human rights must be realised by those whose development is at stake. Human Rights Approaches demand a high quality process, in the faith that the process by which rights are realised is just as significant as the outcome. Human Rights Approaches focus on accountability and identifying those responsible for human rights realisation, whose capacities to meet their responsibilities must be made stronger.

It is human nature or rather nature of any being to aspire for better life. But there has not been common consensus on the issue that what does a 'better' life mean? However in the development discourses in recent few years, concerns have emerged that standard macro-economic statistics, such as GDP, which for a long time had been used as proxies to measure well-being, has been unsuccessful to give a true account of people's present and future living conditions. The financial, social, political, environmental and economic crisis has reinforced this perception and it is now almost accepted that data on GDP provide only a partial viewpoint on the broad range of factors that matter to people's lives and hence new indicators and indexes for measuring well-being as a broad indicator of development is on the move.

This paper tries to bring about relationships among different metrices and tries to capture well-being in different spectrum like peace index, democracy index, human rights risk index, human development, etc. for a few countries around the globe as cases. The methodology is intuitive based on the data compiled from different secondary sources and not statistical tool based. In this paper the central question lies around the fact that whether human rights education can act as a catalyst in bringing better measures of well-being and hence accelerate the developmental process and if yes, how?

The Changing Scenario in Development Paradigm and Role of Human Rights

In 2008, French President Nicolas Sarkozy established the Commission on the Measurement of Economic Performance and Social Progress, chaired and coordinated by Joseph Stiglitz, Amartya Sen and Jean-Paul Fitoussi. In September 2009, the Commission published a report that included around 30 recommendations on how to improve measures of well-being and progress (Stiglitz et al., 2009). At the European level, the European Commission issued a communication on "GDP and beyond" in September 2009, identifying key actions to improve current metrics of progress (EC, 2009).

Defining well-being within a frame is quite challenging because it requires looking at many aspect of people's lives, as well as trying to understand the relative importance of those aspects. Till date a common agreement could not be formed on definition of well-being but majority of the experts and ordinary people around the globe would agree that it requires meeting various human needs together like being in good health, having sound income, as well as the ability to pursue one's goals, to thrive and feel satisfied with their life, ability to enjoy freedom and one's own rights as a human being. Therefore, it is understood that well-being is a complex phenomenon and many of its determinants of well-being are strongly correlated with each other and thus assessing well-being requires a comprehensive framework that includes a large number of components.

While GDP accurately reflects the production of marketed goods and services, it fails to provide a broader measure of social welfare, e.g. voluntary work is not accounted for in standard measures of GDP even though such work can contribute to social well-being as much as paid work. Household production is not included in GDP. Why should the whole day work of a housewife be not accounted in GDP? Why is her pay not even treated as imputed wages? Similarly, the distribution of income is not considered. Two countries with the same GDP per capita may have significantly different income distributions and, consequently, different levels of overall well-being. Moreover, non-economic contributors to well-being are excluded like GDP do not consider the health of a country's citizens, education levels, political participation, or other social and political factors that may significantly affect well-being levels. Considering the depletion and degradation of environmental resources efforts to develop "greener" accounting measures have been taken which was overlooked by standard measure of GDP. Questions are being raised on whether you are money poor or time poor? Do you have time for leisure? There is a wave all around the globe whether in the major three indicators of HDI: income, health and education are sufficient or not to measure well-being. Whether indicators for happiness of citizens, how much the citizens really enjoy freedom in the country or whether they enjoy civil and/or political rights, etc. should also be incorporated.

The OECD's Better Life Initiative, launched in May 2011 following a decade of work on this issue, is a first attempt to bring together internationally comparable measures of well-being in line with the recommendations of the Commission on the Measurement of Economic Performance and Social Progress also known as the Stiglitz-Sen-Fitoussi Commission. The OECD Better Life Initiative includes two main elements: "Your Better Life Index" and "How's Life?" Your Better Life Index (BLI), launched in May 2011, is an interactive tool that allows people to compare countries' performances according to their own preferences in terms of what makes for a better life. First published on 24 May 2011, it includes 11 "dimensions" of well-being: 1. Housing: housing conditions and spendings (e.g. real estate pricing), 2. Income: household income and financial wealth, 3. Jobs: earnings, job security and unemployment,

4. Community: quality of social support network, 5. Education: education and what you get out of it, 6. Environment: quality of environment (e.g. environmental health), 7. Governance: involvement in democracy, 8. Health, 9. Life Satisfaction: level of happiness, 10. Safety: murder and assault rates, 11. Work-life balance.

According to the 2000 Human Development Report human rights and human development share a common vision and a common purpose—to secure, for every human being, freedom, well-being and dignity. The Report says that Human freedom is the common purpose and common motivation of human rights and human development. Achieving rights for all people in all countries will require action and commitment from the major players in society. On the other hand, the 2013 Human Development Report identifies four specific areas of focus for sustaining development momentum: enhancing equity, including on the gender dimension; enabling greater voice and participation of citizens, including youth; confronting environmental pressures; and managing demographic change. It is interesting that the primary agenda for more than a decade has revolved around human rights in various facets a stimulus of development process.

A Reflection of Some Linkages Among the New Indicators of Well-being

There is no clear cut blueprint for measuring human wellbeing, but around the world there are a growing number of examples of increasingly well developed approaches for bringing well-being into national public policy debate. This includes the development of conceptual frameworks and work to develop new approaches to measuring human well-being. Since the Istanbul Declaration at the OECD Global Forum of 2007, which committed signatories to work towards the development of appropriate indicators of societal progress, there have been extensive debates around how to incorporate new measures of well-being in public policy processes.

Democracy is one of the universal core values and principles of the United Nations. Respect for human rights and fundamental freedoms and the principle of holding periodic and genuine elections by universal suffrage are essential elements of democracy. These values are embodied in the Universal Declaration of Human Rights and further developed in the International Covenant on Civil and Political Rights which enshrine a host of political rights and civil liberties supporting meaningful democracies. Democracy and human rights are interrelated. The greatest protection of human rights emanates from a democratic framework grounded in the rule of law. A functional democracy that accommodates diversity is increasingly becoming the best bet in the globe against the concentration of power in the hands of a few and the abuse that inevitably results from it. The principle that 'all power ultimately rests with the people and must be exercised with their consent' lies at the heart of democracy. Democracy is premised on the recognition and protection of people's right to have a say in all decision-making processe which itself is based on the central principle of 'equality of all human beings'. As Mahatma Gandhi had pointed out "My notion of democracy is that under it the weakest should have the same opportunity as the strongest."

The rights enshrined in the International Covenant on Economic, Social and Cultural Rights and subsequent human rights instruments covering group rights (e.g. indigenous peoples, minorities, persons with disabilities), are equally essential for democracy as they ensure an equitable distribution of wealth, and equality and equity in respect of access to civil and political rights. (United Nations)

In this section, the purpose is to find inter-relationships of a few indicators and indexes beyond GDP with some cases of countries from the globe. In Table 1 a few countries with largest discrepancy between democracy and peace have been presented along with Human Rights Risk. The table clearly reflects that almost all democracy deficit and peace deficit countries around the globe, are in either extreme human rights risk zone or high risk zone except United States which is in medium risk zone. Thus countries which are democracy deficit and peace deficit are unable to ensure human rights to its citizens.As per the index, factors that mostly contribute in risk prone countries as far as human rights are concerned are repression of freedom of speech; ethnic and sectarian conflicts; a lack of worker protection; and competition for land and water between local populations and industrial business user.

Table 1: Countries with largest discrepancy between democracy and peace along with Human Rights Risk

Democracy Deficit	Human Rights Risk Index 2014	Peace Deficit	Human Rights Risk
Qatar	Extreme Risk	Israel	High Risk
Laos	High Risk	India	Extreme Risk
UAE	High Risk	Colombia	Extreme Risk
Vietnam	High Risk	South Africa	High Risk
Oman	High Risk	Mexico	Extreme Risk
Bhutan	Medium Risk	Jamaica	High Risk
Kuwait	Extreme Risk	United States	Medium Risk
Djibouti	Extreme Risk	Thailand	High Risk
Jordan	High Risk	Philippines	Extreme Risk
Equatorial Guinea	High Risk	Peru	High Risk

Source: Compiled by researcher from Global Peace Index Report 2014 and the map of Human Rights Risk Index 2014 of Maplecroft

Findings of the 41st edition of 'Freedom in the World', the oldest, most authoritative report of democracy and human rights, reports that fifty-four countries showed overall declines in political rights and civil liberties, compared with 40 that showed gains. For the eighth consecutive year, Freedom in the World recorded more declines in democracy worldwide than gains. Table 2 portrays the freedom index for the countries that were considered in Table 1 as cases. The table shows the nature of freedom and the score on political and civil rights. While score of 1 reflects best situation, a score of 7 is the worst. It is observed that while countries like Qatar, Laos, UAE, Vietnam, Djibouti, Jordan, Equatorial Guinea along being democracy deficit are also not free in terms of civil and political rights, Bhutan and Kuwait show a better picture. On the contrary the countries which are deficit in peace (as shown in Table 1) have better scores in freedom except Columbia, Mexico, Thailand and Philippines. Thus, very broadly it may be said that democracy and enjoyment of civil and political rights are better correlated based on findings of sample countries.

Table 2: Freedom Index

Country	Freedom	PR	CL	Country	Freedom	PR	CL
Qatar	Not Free	6	5	Israel	Free	1	2
Laos	Not Free	7	6	India	Free	2	3
UAE	Not Free	6	6	Colombia	Partly Free	3	4
Vietnam	Not Free	7	5	South Africa	Free	2	2
Oman	Not Free	6	5	Mexico	Partly Free	3	3
Bhutan	Partly Free	3	4	Jamaica	Free	2	3
Kuwait	Partly Free	5	5	United State	Free	1	1
Djibouti	Not Free	6	5	Thailand	Partly Free	4	4
Jordan	Not Free	6	5	Philippines	Partly Free	3	3
Equatorial Guinea	Not Free	7	7	Peru	Free	2	3

Note: PR and CL stand for political rights and civil liberties, respectively; 1 represents the most free and 7 the least free rating. The ratings reflect global events from January 1, 2013, through December 31, 2013.

Source: Compiled by researcher from 41st edition of Freedom in the World available at www.freedomhouse.org/report/freedom-world/freedom-world-2014

In Table 3 three more indicators have been added to Global Peace Index of 2014 and Democracy Index of 2012. These indicators are cost of violence containment as a percentage of GDP, level of human development and population size. It is interesting to note from the table that countries with lower global peace in most cases have higher cost of violence containment as a percentage of GDP. No direct relationship however was observed between population size and peace index, democracy index or level of development because it was observed that a country like Israel which has low global peace index but higher democracy index with medium population size has very high level of human development. On the other hand country like United States with very large population show very high level of human development but medium level of global peace along with high score in democracy. However among the sample countries, the cost of violence containment as a percentage of

GDP is the maximum for United States. An interesting case is of Laos with high peace index but very poor democracy index.

Table 3: Some other indicators of development

Country	2014 Global Peace Index rank	2012 Democracy Index Rank	Cost of Violence Containment as a % of GDP	Level of Human Development	Population Size
INDIA	143/162 [Low]	38/167 [World's biggest democracy]	3.6	Medium	Very Large
BHUTAN	16/162 [Very High]	107/167	0.5	Medium	Small
QATAR	22/162 [Very High]	138/167	3.1	Very High	Small
LAOS	38/162 [High]	156/167	1.8	Medium	Medium
UAE	40/162 [High]	149/167	4.3	Very High	Medium
VIETNAM	45/162 [High]	144/167	3.8	Medium	Large
EQUATORIAL GUINEA	93/162 [Medium]	160/167	44	Medium	Small
ISRAEL	149/162 (Low)	37/167	8.1	Very High	Medium
COLOMBIA	150/162 (Low)	57/167	9.7	High	Large
PERU	119/162 (Medium)	61/167	4.5	High	Large
SOUTH AFRICA	122/162 (Medium)	31/167	8.6	Medium	Large
MEXICO	138/162 (Low)	51/167	9.4	High	Very Large
UNITED STATES	101/162 (Medium)	21/167 (Full democracy)	10.2	Very High	Very Large

Source: Compiled from Peace Index 2014,OECD Reports.

Therefore from the tables it is observed that one indicator alone is not enough to portray the situation of 'well-being' of its citizens. It is felt that though they are interlinked and for some countries a few indicators are quite satisfactory but, there is a huge deficit around the globe as far as enjoying human rights are concerned.

Possibility and Role of Human Right Education in the New Trail of Development

"The World Conference on Human Rights considers human rights education, training and public information essential for the promotion and achievement of stable and harmonious relations among communities and for fostering mutual understanding, tolerance and peace" (Vienna Declaration and Programme of Action, Part II-D, para. 78). The international community is increasingly adopting intergovernmental framework at the global level, such as the World Programme for Human Rights Education (from 2005 onwards), which aims at encouraging the development of sustainable national strategies and programmes in human rights education. This international trend highlights a consensus that the education system plays a vital role in fostering respect, participation, equality and non-discrimination in our societies. For the education system to play such a role, a comprehensive approach to implementing human rights education, addressing not only educational policies, processes and tools but also the environment within which education takes place, is needed (Plan of action, World Programme on Human Rights Education, 2006).

The Dakar Framework for Action on Education for All: Meeting Our Collective Commitments, adopted at the World Education Forum, reaffirmed a vision of education supported by the Universal Declaration of Human Rights and the Convention on the Rights of the Child and geared towards learning to live together. In the Dakar Framework, education is considered key "to sustainable development and peace and stability", by fostering social cohesion and empowering people to become active participants in social transformation.

Human rights education as a means of social transformation and a stimulus of development is defined as training, dissemination, and information efforts aimed at building a universal culture of human rights by imparting knowledge and skills, and molding attitudes. Human rights education basically has five dimensions:

- strengthening respect for the human personality and its dignity;
- fully developing the human personality and its dignity;

- promoting understanding, tolerance, gender equality, and friendship among all nations, indigenous peoples, and racial, national, ethnic, religious, and linguistic groups;
- enabling all persons to participate effectively in a free society; and
- furthering the activities of the United Nations to maintain peace (Guidelines for national plans of action for human rights education—United Nations).

Article 30 of the UDHR declares that one goal of education should be "the strengthening of respect for human rights and fundamental freedoms". According to the International Covenant on Civil and Political Rights (ICCPR), a government "may not stand in the way of people's learning about (their rights)". In 2013 the World Bank Group announced that it would focus on two overarching measurable goals: ending extreme poverty by 2030 and promoting shared prosperity (2014 World Development Indicators, World bank). One of the means of promoting shared prosperity is through education.

It is universally accepted that education is the best source of social mobility, equality, and empowerment, both at the individual and collective levels. Further, it is considered as a precondition for a healthy democratic society. It is thus important that education includes the study of peace, human rights, and democracy as essential to society's development.

The goal of development is no longer seen as industrialisation and economic growth but as the greatest possible fulfilment of all human rights for as many people as possible. The central concern of development is therefore no longer the economy but human beings (Human Rights Manual). Hence, there is a huge need to fill the gap where each and every human being is not aware of his/her rights. The acceleration in this process or perhaps the only major solution for the process in fostering Human Rights Education in all forms at different levels.

Figure 1 tries to illustrate the role of human rights education in development by demonstrating what are the indicators of well-being, types of human rights education, the process and the components that need to be incorporated for human rights education. While well-being as a measure of development may be measured in three different dimensions: material and physical condition, quality of life, rights enjoyed encompassing various indicators as shown in Fig. 1, the implementation of human

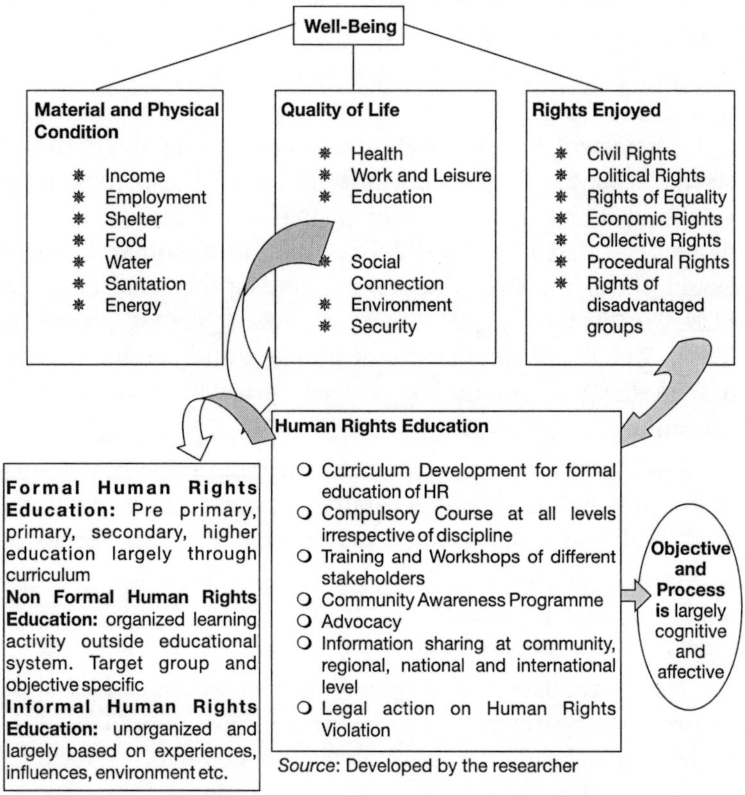

Source: Developed by the researcher

Fig. 1: Role of HR Education in development and well-being

rights education for well-being need not be only formal education but also informal and non-formal methods of education. Largely the objectives and process of human rights education are cognitive and affective in nature but in many situations go beyond it and hence the curriculum needs to be developed in such a way that learners can relate the learning with whatever they see around, whatever they do around and finally there is a positive modification in behaviour. Thus, human rights education in this process can encourage in betterment of life by understanding the rights enjoyed and hence claiming those rights and respecting the rights of others as well so that the globe becomes a better place to live in.

Concluding Comments

Thus, human rights education is education, training and information aimed at building a universal culture of human rights through the distribution of knowledge, imparting of skills and shaping of attitudes to prompt action directed at strengthening respect for human rights, fundamental freedoms, tolerance, equality and peace, among individuals, within societies and among nations which in turn may help in fostering well-being.

Such a system of education requires the adoption of a human rights-based approach to education, which promotes both—human rights *through* education, ensuring that all the components and processes of education—including curricula, materials, methods and training—are conducive to the learning of human rights, and human rights in education, ensuring that the human rights of all members of the community are respected and human rights are practised within the education system.

Human rights education goes beyond cognitive learning and includes the social and emotional development of all those involved in the learning and teaching process. It aims at developing a culture of human rights. To this end, it is essential to ensure that human rights teaching and learning happen in a human rights-based learning environment. It is essential to ensure that educational objectives, practices and the organization of the learning environment whether formal, informal or non-formal are consistent with human rights values and principles. Likewise, it is important that the culture and the community within and beyond the learning environment are also embedding those principles. A rights-based approach for human rights education is characterized by mutual understanding, respect and responsibility. It fosters equal opportunities, a sense of belonging, autonomy, dignity and self-esteem for all members of the community.

Thus the new development paradigm along with incorporation of various spectrum of human well-being in the form of indicators need to pay attention to a human rights education based approach to development process. It needs to look beyond the scope of formal education and regional constraints but requires to take a holistic approach so that the future citizens of this global world are well equipped with the knowledge of human rights and enjoy their own human rights and in turn have fullest respect for others human rights which goes beyond all boundaries of region, caste, creed, sex, religion etc.

The scourge of war, conflict, high level of human rights risk zones around the globe, rising cost of violence containment as a percentage of GDP throws a stern warning that we shall once again find ourselves painfully ill equipped to meet the challenge of an adult world of tomorrow, unless we are determined to lay foundations in the education process through the compulsory introduction of human rights education. The key to the salvation of mankind lies in reorientation of the mind of the people where human rights education can act as a principal catalyst.

REFERENCES

Commonwealth Expert Group in Democracy and Development http://www.thecommonwealth.org/shared_asp_files/uploadedfiles/{3BB5DD0B-926A-4DBB-82B6-14D55AF2F622}_34591%20 Text.pdf

European Commission available at http://ec.europa.eu/atwork/key-documents/index_en.htm

Global Peace Index 2014, Institute for economics and Peace available at http://www.visionofhumanity.org/sites/default/files/2014%20 Global%20Peace%20Index%20REPORT.pdf

Helliwell, J.F. (2005). Well-Being, Social Capital and Public Policy: What's New? NBER Working Paper No. 11807.

Human Rights Manual available at http://www.entwicklung.at/uploads/media/HUMAN_RIGHTS_Manual__July_2010.pdf Lewis. W.A. (1955). *The Theory of Economic Growth*. Taylor and Francis: London.

Human Rights Risk Index Map of Maplecroft available at https://maplecroft.com/themes/hr

Human Development Report 2000 available at hdr.undp.org/en/content/human-development-report-2000

Human Development Report 2013 available at hdr.undp.org/sites/default/files/reports/14/hdr2013_en_complete.pdf

OECD (2011). How's Life?: Measuring well-being, OECD Publishing. http://dx.doi.org/10.1787/9789264121164-en

OECD (2013). Proceedings: 4th World Forum on Statistics, Knowledge and Policy Measuring Well-Being for Development and Policy Making, New Delhi. http://www.oecd.org/site/worldforumindia/OECD-World-Forum-2012-India-proceedings

Plan of action, World Programme on Human Rights Education, 2006 available at http://unesdoc.unesco.org/images/0014/001478/147853e.pdf

Stiglitz, J.E., S. Amartya, and J. Fitoussi (2009). The measurement of economic performance and social progress revisited. Documents de Travail de l'OFCE 2009-33, Observatoire Francais des Conjonctures Economiques (OFCE).

The Human Rights Education Handbook: Effective Practices for Learning, Action, and Change; Nancy Flowers with Marcia Bernbaum, Kristi RudeliusPalmer and Joel Tolman, Human Rights Resource Center, University of Minnesota; 2000.

The Universal Declaration of Human Rights available at http://www.un.org/en/documents/udhr

United Nations Educational, Scientific and Cultural Organization, Final Report of the World Education Forum, Dakar, Senegal, 26-28 April 2000, Paris, 2000.

UNESCO, "Education for Sustainability: from Rio to Johannesburg: lessons learned from a decade of commitment" (Paris, 2002).

Universal Declaration of Human Rights; preamble.

Vienna Declaration and Programme of Action; available at http://www.ohchr.org/EN/ProfessionalInterest/Pages/Vienna.aspx

"What are human rights?"; OHCHR; available www.ohchr.org/en/issues/Pages/WhatareHumanRights.aspx

"What are human rights?"; New Zealand Human Rights Commission; available at www.hrc.co.nz/human-rights-environment/what-are-human-rights

World Development Indicators 2014, World bank, http://data.worldbank.org/sites/default/files/wdi-2014-book.pdf

10

Gender Disparity in Education of Muslim Girls: A Study of Facts and Illusions in India

Azra Abidi

All over the world the movement for improving women's status has always emphasized education as the most significant instrument. The National Policy on Education (NPE, 1992) in India is a landmark in the approach to women's education. It has attempted for the first time to address itself to the basic issues of women's equality. In India, gender disparities persist in the enrolment rates between boys and girls at all levels. Gender inequality has become a major issue in India in the recent years. This paper discusses gender disparities in the education of Muslim girls in the country. It identifies and analyses various factors that cause gender inequality in education. Further, it also provides some policy implications to solve the gender-related problems in the country. The present paper also deals the provisions mentioned in the Constitution and law of our country which not only grants equality to women but also empowers the State to adopt measures of positive discrimination in favor of women for neutralizing the cumulative socio-economic, education and political disadvantages faced by them.

EDUCATION OF WOMEN IN ISLAM

The term education is mentioned in Islam as an instrument to mould the personality of human being as well as it is for the entire humanity. So we can say that education in Islam is for all, not specifically for male or for female and below mentioned purposes of education can support my words that—

1. It is prime responsibility of each individual to seek knowledge and it is a sacred duty; it is obligatory on every Muslim, male and female.
2. The subject matter of education in Islam is man as a man. In Islam human being is not considered as machine or instrument.
3. Education in Islam is a comprehensive whole, an education which brings about a harmonious development of mind, body and soul.
4. Development of moral character is the first and foremost object of the Islamic system of education.
5. Islamic education is belief oriented and mental.
6. The focus of education in Islam is both on moral as well as on knowledge and wisdom. In Islam the system of education is unbiased and liberal.

The above-mentioned points are showing textual condition but contextual situation is different. It is not only in our country at the global level, there is a gender disparity regarding education among Muslim girls. The gender gap, drop out and discrimination is very high particularly related to formal education in different institutions.

Gender Inequality at Global Level

The restrictive effect of traditional sex roles, socialization in the family has its parallel in educational practices in educational institutions traditionally. Most educational fields remain sex typed, a phenomenon that compounds the occupational stratification by sex. Further, sex-biased educational practices, differential curricula and textbooks perpetuate the traditional division of labour between sexes. This limits not only the range of occupations chosen by women but also lands them in low ranking occupations corresponding to their assisting roles in the household. Thus, traditionally education has contributed to educational and occupational stratification between the sexes by encouraging and preparing girls to pursue an extremely limited number of traditionally feminine roles. High level of sex segregation exists in the work force and women enter a limited number of feminine sex stereotyped occupations, which are also low in status.

The lives of girls and women continue to be controlled by the patriarchal belief systems and structures, which use prescriptions and proscriptions to keep women in their place. All decisions are taken by men and all assets are owned by them. The process of gender discrimination begins even before birth and continues throughout the life of a female. Besides women and girls do more work than males but get much less than their legitimate share in food, health, education and training. The traditional socialization practices of a society with a marked son preference are highly discriminatory to the girl child not only in matters of food, health care, education and play but also succeed in making her believe that she is inferior and less competent than her male counterparts.

UNESCO Education For All (EFA) report on the elimination of gender disparities in enrolments raise many questions for governments and civil societies in developing countries. It is reported that 57 per cent of the estimated 104 million children in the 5-10 years age group who are out of school worldwide are believed to be girls. The enrolment of girls in many countries is only three-fourths that of boys. Eliminating gender disparities in primary and secondary education by 2005 and ensuring gender equality by 2015. The report cautions that the 2015 deadline for achieving 50 per cent improvement in adult literacy and universal primary education may remain a dream for one-third of the world's population. The 164 national governments that adopted the Dakar Framework of Action at the World Education Forum in Senegal in 2000 committed themselves to putting in place policies to facilitate these goals. The international community also held out the assurance that resources would not be a constraint. But the EFA report notes that aid flows have been disappointingly low in recent years. Paradoxically, this comes at a time when the accent on primary education has been high on the agenda of many developing countries. The gender inequality is indeed prevalent in many developing countries like

India. However, the persistence of this gender inequality in the arena of children's education must not be treated as inevitable.

Further, according to Global Crisis Solution Center, some two-thirds of the 130 million children in the world currently not in school are girls. This means that about 86.7 million girls are out of school. UNICEF report indicates that the number of girls out of school in sub-Saharan Africa rose over the last decade from 20 million in 1990 to 24 million in 2002.

Educational Development of Muslim Girls in India

During ancient times and middle ages, education in the Indian subcontinent remained in general the monopoly of higher castes; women's education was usually not encouraged. In India, the Turkish Queen Razia Sultana, other Muslim queens and princesses like Noor Jehan, Mumtaz Mahal and Jahanara wielded political and military power. However, the colonial period and industrial revolution showed a marked downtrend in the status of Muslim women but their status dipped after the wars. This is because the Muslim community, whose governments had fallen, felt endangered and threatened by the Western culture and now wanted to hold on rigidly to their own identity. With breakup of the Muslim empire after the two wars, Muslims wished to preserve their past glory somewhat as they saw at the centre of the Western culture, a misused, overworked and undressed women as its symbol. They reacted in a natural and protective way by restricting their own women from external influences and even curbing their legitimate rights including right to education at times. This trend gradually became a custom and a practice, resulting finally in illiterate, ignorant and custom-bound timid Muslim women.

Khwaja Altaf Husain Hali's 1905 novel *Chup Ki Dad* (*Voices of the Silent*) vividly captured the reality of women's oppression. Hali argued for female education; although he felt this should be imparted at home. Mumtaz Ali and his wife Mohammadi Begum founded a newspaper *Tahzib-un-Niswan* (*Women's Reformer*) which took up the issues of female education. Ameer Ali, a Bengali lawyer, author of the celebrated *The Spirit of Islam* (1922) argued against polygamy and emphasized the need for reform in Muslim law. Rokeya Shakhawat Hossain from Bengal an advocate of social reform—spoke out against the 'excessive absurdities' of female seclusion. She was one of the few whose concerns included the bulk of poor, uneducated Muslim women.

Individual and collective efforts notwithstanding, modernist views regarding education for Muslim women were not without their contradictions. Syed Ahmed Khan urged Muslims to gain a modern secular education. However, his vision of modern education for Muslims did not include women. Mohammed Iqbal, the renowned poet and philosopher, was also quite averse to the idea of female education. The ulema favoured women's education but only insofar as it centered on religion (i.e. the Qur'an), family values and the moral virtue of women. In his classic text *Beheshti Zewar* (*Heavenly Ornaments*), Maulana Ashraf Ali Thanawi delineated domestic roles for women in great detail.

Despite pressures of religious orthodoxies, social prejudice and class/gender bias, Muslim women at the start of the twentieth century successfully emerged from the isolation of traditional roles as self-aware individuals, determined to claim a greater role in public affairs. The theme of women's education was taken up by all communities including Muslims. This topic was first raised at the "All-Male Muslim Educational Congress" in 1896 and in subsequent years there were vigorous attempts by Muslim women to lobby for women's education and entry in politics. In 1906, Sheikh Abdullah and his wife Wahid Jahan Begum established a separate school for girls at Aligarh. 'Purdahnashin Madarsa'—a school for girls in seclusion in Calcutta—was established in 1913; The Begum of Bhopal, Sultan Jahan Begum. The activities of Anjuman-e-Himayat-e-Islam, Lahore opened a new chapter in Muslim women's education in the north in the first quarter of the 20th century she founded a girls' school in 1914. The name of Maulvi S. Karamat Husain, the founder of Karamt Husain Girls' College, Lucknow also cannot be overlooked in this regard. There were reform movements that worked for the emancipation of women, fighting the system of pardah, polygamy and child marriage amongst Muslims in western and southern India. Badruddin Tyabji (1844-1906) was the most outstanding leader of these movements—one of the founders of the Indian National Congress and its third president. Muslim women began entering educational institutions for the first time. Yet, as a scholar observes, it was not easy to dislodge deeply entrenched social mores, "At the Mohammedan co-educational college at Madras, girls were required to wear their burqas (veils) and at Aligarh male teachers sat behind a curtain."

The Main Reasons for Gender Gap in the Education of Muslim Girls

With Independence, time came to review the whole educational process. The Constitution accordingly included a provision making education compulsory for all children up to the age of 14. The Muslim community was unable to take the maximum advantage of the opportunity provided by the state, because of an unsympathetic official attitude, communally surcharged national climate and its own confusion in fixing up priorities. Therefore, the Muslim community was left with the only choice of extensive voluntary efforts for elevating their educational status. Southern States realized the hard reality first. Besides societies and associations which promoted education among Muslims, there were the same philanthropists that were responsible for giving a fillip to education.

As we have noted earlier, girl's education developed largely through private initiative in the pre-independence period and the State started taking interest only in the 1880s. Several education commissions and committees set up by the British rulers took cognizance of the need to educate girls and women in the larger interest of the society. After independence, several committees and commissions have been set up from time to time on education, some exclusively for women's education, which as we shall notice later, has changed substantially over the last six decades.

The National Council for Women's Education which was set up by the Ministry of Education, following one of the main recommendations of the National Committee on Women's Education, at its thirteenth meeting held in 1974 made important recommendations for the education of women, through formal and non-formal channels.

The Report of the Committee on Status of Women in India (CSWI): Towards equality was placed before the Parliament in 1975. The Committee examined the constitutional, legal and administrative provisions which had a bearing on the status of women and noted with concern poor female literacy, the declining sex ratio, and declining work participation rates, concentration of women in low paid occupations and that women were deprived of basic needs of health, nutrition, education and employment and were in a situation of total powerlessness with no share in decision-making processes.

Education of Girls and Women in the Five-Year Plans: Different five-year plan observed the need of girls education and that was mentioned on priority basis in five years plans. Meanwhile it was only in late seventies that backwardness of education of Muslim minority started receiving attention and resulted in some action on the part of the state. The minorities' commission was set up in 1978. It was a non-statutory body until 1992, when parliament enacted the national commission.

For minorities the first statutory commission was set up in 1993, called the National Commission for Minorities (NCM). However, it is only after Census 2001 brought out its first Religion report that statistics on several aspects of population by religion (literacy, educational attainment, sex ratio, work participation) became available in the public domain that has led to public debate and action. A high power panel appointed by the Ministry of Home Affairs and headed by Dr. Gopal Singh identified Muslims and neo-Buddhists as two educationally backward minorities at the national level and proposed that special efforts have to be made to bring the educationally backward minorities on par with rest of the society. Forty-four districts with concentration of Muslim minority were identified for special attention based on 1981 census.

- **In May 1983**, former Prime Minister Indira Gandhi issued a 15-point directive on welfare of Minorities. The 15-point programme for minorities was announced in 1983. The national policy on education, 1986 and revised programme of action 1992 need to take special steps to advance education of Muslims was noted in the National Policy of Education 1986 its programme of action (revised in 1992) and led to formulation of the area. Intensive educational development as a Central Government scheme of the MHRD.

- **In 2003**, an important work was done by Prof. Zoya Hasan and Ritu Menon on Muslim girl's education in five cities. Delhi, Aligarh, Hyderabad, Kolkata and Calicut. The research showed a dismal state of Muslim female education as well as the efforts being made by several Muslim social activists in different parts of India to address the issue. They claim that over 75% of Muslim women in India are illiterate, literacy being officially defined rather generously to include just about anyone who can read and write a sentence or two. The situation in the northern states, especially in rural areas, is said to be particularly dismal. 85% of rural north Indian Muslim women are unable to read or write.
- **In 2005**, the Prime Minister's high level committee on social, economic and educational status of Muslim Community (Sachar Committee) in India was set up under the chairmanship of Justice Rajinder Sachar which submitted its report in 2006. This committee noted with concern the low socio-economic status of Muslim minority, higher poverty, lower literacy and educational attainments, higher unemployment rates, lower availability of infrastructure and lower participation in decision making, in civil services including police, judiciary and in elected bodies, and above, all perceived sense of insecurity and discrimination.
- **In 2007**, a study was conducted by Usha Nayar and she found in her research that Muslim girls and women lag behind their male counterparts. Gender disparity in literacy rates is 9.67% in rural and 13.11% in urban areas. Only 3.6% Muslims are graduates as compared to

the National Average of 6.7%. Mean Years of Schooling (MYS) for 7-16 years of age in 2001 was 3.9 years. In that it was 3.26 years for Muslims and 2.7 years for Muslim girls. Findings of the study revealed the educational backwardness of Muslims and confirmed the unequal status of women.

- **In 2008**, a report by the NCM (National Commission on Minorities) titled 'Socio-economic Status of Notified Minority Communities (Christians, Sikhs, Buddhists and Parsis) except Muslims' says that the minority communities—apart from the Muslims—have a literacy rate higher than the average literacy rate of the country.

The Constitution of India grants Muslims and other minorities equality of status and opportunities with other citizens to accelerate the process of educational and socio-economic justice. The Constitution of India grants the rights to Equality and Right to Freedom of Religion and Protection of Interest of Minorities in regard to educational rights. The above-mentioned studies and work shows different perspective on Muslim women education in India. We can come to this conclusion that in post-Independence society the educational status of Muslim girls are not satisfactory. On the completion of six decades of independence, women in Muslim communities face considerable challenges as citizens of India and as members of India's largest minority. According to government reports, Muslim women are among the poorest, educationally disenfranchised, economically vulnerable, politically marginalized group in the country.

Important Constitutional and Legal Provisions for Muslim Women in India

In post-Independence India, a large number of constitutional and legislative measures and many forward looking policies and programmes have been directed at integrating women in the mainstream of national development. The State guarantees equal opportunities to women and forbids discrimination in all matters relating to employment and appointment to any public office. Under the protective discrimination clause, the State has passed several social and labour legislation and drawn up special programmes and schemes for the protection, welfare and development of women. There are laws to protect women from hazardous work; laws providing maternity benefits and child care services, and equal wages for work. Additionally, women have reserved quotas and seats in many educational and training institutions, development schemes, and local bodies and in government jobs.

India has one of the most impressive sets of laws for women and girls and yet little is known about them either by women themselves or by men. Laws in India by and large cover the women belonging to each and every religious community. However, there is one notable exception. This is in the realm of personal laws that is the laws governing marriage, divorce, inheritance, child custody and maintenance, etc. Since different religious communities display wide variations in their personal beliefs and customs, it was considered appropriate to respect the differences and make personal laws commensurate with the customary practices within each community. These laws have been framed keeping in mind the varied religious beliefs, since India is a multi-religious country.

CONSTITUTIONAL AND LEGAL PROVISIONS

The Constitution of India not only grants equality to women but also empowers the State to adopt measures of positive discrimination in favor of women for neutralizing the cumulative socio-economic, education and political disadvantages faced by them. Fundamental rights, among others, ensure equality before the law and equal protection of law; prohibits discrimination against any citizen on grounds of religion, race, caste, sex or place of birth, and guarantee equality of opportunity to all citizens in matters relating to employment. Articles 14, 15, 15(3), 16, 39(a), 39(b), 39(c) and 42 of the Constitution are of specific importance in this regard.

To uphold the constitutional mandate, the State has enacted various legislative measures intended to ensure equal rights, to counter social discrimination and various forms of violence and atrocities and to provide support services especially to working women. Although women may be victims of any of the crimes such as ‘Murder’, ‘Robbery’, ‘Cheating’, etc., the crimes, which are directed specifically against women, are characterized as ‘Crime against Women’.

Steps to be Taken to Improve Muslim Girls’ Participation in the Schools

India now has half a century’s experience in dealing with sharp inequalities and disparities rooted in several millennia of its evolution, yet we still see sharp inequalities of caste, creed, tribe and rural urban divide. Gender cuts across all these layers making women and girls of the disadvantaged groups the most deprived members of our society. Gender disparities in educational and all other social and demographic indicators reflect the unequal position of girls and women in a highly sexist, gender discriminatory social order. I can suggest some important points to improve the educational condition of Muslim girls:

1. The government should take immediate steps to fill the gap of educational facilities being offered for Muslim girls as citizen of this country.
2. The government should collect data on Muslim girl’s educational status including dropout rates.
3. Activists, organizations and policymakers should make the data available to the general public and for use. Such information would need to be quantitative, qualitative as well as comparative, so that conditions between Muslims and other communities can be compared and policies suitably adjusted to ensure equity.
4. Much emphasis should be given to make the data keeping in terms with gender, region, class, caste; linguistic groups, etc. so that all the Muslims are not treated as a monolith.
5. Development schemes by the government should allocate resources in Muslim-dominated localities on a scale proportionate to their population; it should be suitably made and implemented.

6. Development schemes must also be culturally sensitive so that they are acceptable to the Muslim community. For instance, enforced co-education after a certain level or Hinduised or anti-Muslim biases in textbooks often act as a major hindrance to Muslim, particularly Muslim girls' education. These issues need to be sensitively addressed and approached.
7. In planning and implementing development schemes, the participation of the local community, including Muslims and other marginalized groups, must be ensured.
8. Civil society or NGOs should take a proactive action in the Muslim-dominated areas of Delhi and make their presence felt.
9. Sensitization of religious Ulema to mobilize parents for their girl's education is a need of Muslim community. So that they can help and mobilize public through their lectures and literature.
10. Dialogue on Muslim social, economic and educational issues also needs to be initiated with the media, politicians, bureaucrats, and non-governmental organizations.
11. In order to improve the educational status of the Muslim minorities, efforts has to be made to improve their socio-economic status as well.
12. Muslim girls are the last to be sent to schools and in adversity, the first to be pulled out of schools. This condition essays their vulnerability and no say in decision making.
13. It is also very important that Muslim women and their family members should be aware towards their constitutional and legal rights.
14. Government should organize legal awareness camp in the Muslim locality to sensitize women, girls, male counterparts as well as Ulema (religious leaders) to discuss Muslim women's education.

Conclusion

Different studies on Muslim women and girls education show that educational backwardness of Muslim is not only a reason of religion or demography, but a reflection of the socio-economic status of a community, in a certain region or state. The alarmingly high dropout rate of girls after secondary school owes to several factors including gender disparity, poverty, and lack of separate girls' schools, early marriage and community resistance. Another major difficulty is the problem of finding appropriate husbands for highly educated Muslim girls. Considerable opposition to co-education exists, as parents feel this might lead girls astray. Many families tend to withdraw their girls from education after high school for fear of girls' safety, especially if colleges are located far from their homes. While all teachers and parents believe in the importance of girls' education but the Madrasa teachers stress that the ideal education that Muslim girls should receive is religious, plus modicum of general subjects that can enable them to become good housewives. There is disappointment, particularly among Muslims regarding the failure of various government-funded schemes ostensibly meant for minority education as well as the routine harassment that Muslim educational institutions seeking recognition and grants-in-aid are subjected to in many states. Religious leaders do not see any use for giving formal education to girls and who feel that Dini Taleem (religious education) is enough for girls.

It is observed that the persistent denial of equal opportunity of education to the Muslim girls of our country is due to religious, traditional and cultural beliefs and attitudes. Cultural stigmas promote negative attitudes and habits in men and women that pass from the generation-to-generation and family to the workplace. Furthermore, it is not compatible to the policy of the Government of India (GoI) that clearly stipulates equal opportunities of education and employment to both men and women. Another reason which I want to mention here is that most of the Muslim women are not aware towards their constitutional rights, GoI schemes for minorities or law which support them. So this is another related problem of their educational backwardness in India.

Indeed, educational disparity retards the advancement of women as well as the progress and development of a nation. The emancipation of women and the achievement of equality between men and women are essential to India's development and the transformation of its citizens. The elimination of discrimination against women is a social, political, legal and moral imperative that must ultimately reshape existing economic, social and cultural arrangements. Promoting the entry of greater numbers of women into education and training as well as positions of prominence and authority is of paramount importance in the country.

It is a responsibility of every citizen, parents, as well as the community and different institutions including judiciary to play due role in alleviating the problems specifically hindering girls from schooling. In addition the Ministry of Education, Ministry of HRD and Women Commission should take on panel some of the emerging issues in gender inequality in education of Muslim community and provide the basis for an action plan. This kind of action plan can minimize the gender disparity specifically in the educational field for the better future of Muslim girls.

REFERENCES

Alam, Arshad (2006), "Beyond Rhetoric: Understanding Contemporary Madrasas," *Islam and Muslim Societies: A Social Science Journal*, Vol. 2, No. 6, New Delhi.

Bhatty, Zarina (ed), "Status of Muslim Women and Social Change, Indian Women: From Purdah to Modernity", Vikas Publishing House, New Delhi, 1976.

DISE Analytical Report 2007-08 by Arun C. Mehta, NUEPA, New Delhi-16.

Education of Muslim Girls: A Study of the Area Intensive Programme by Anita Nuna; Deptt. of Women's' Studies, NCERT, New Delhi-16.

Elementary Education in India, Where do we stand? By Arun C. Mehta; District Report Cards 2006-07, 2007-08, NUEPA, New Delhi-16.

Hasan, Zoya and Menon, Ritu (2004), "Unequal Citizens, A Study of Muslim Women in India," Oxford University Press, New Delhi.

Metcalf, Barbara Daly (1995), "Too Little and Too Much: Reflections on Muslims in the History of India," *Journal of Asian Studies*, Vol. 54, No. 4.

Muslim Female Education in Metropolitan City of Calcutta—A perspective Study of an Urban Minority (1971-81) by Santimay Ray; Ministry of Human Resource Development, Deptt. of Education, New Delhi.

Minority Education in India: Issues of Access, Equity and Inclusion by Abdul Waheed; Serials Publications, 2010.

Muslims in India, Volume III by Aijazuddin Ahmad; under Hamdard Education Society; Inter-India Publications, 1995.

Robinson, Rowena (2007), "Marginalization and Violence: Concerns for India and Its Muslims," *Social Action*, Vol. 57, No. 3, New Delhi, p. 233.

Rokaiya Begum: "Education and Muslim, Women in Rural West Bengal" in M.A. Siddiqui (ed), *Muslims in Free India: Their Social Profile and Problems*, New Delhi: Institute of Objective Studies, 1998.

Sekh Rahim Mondal's: Educational Status of Muslims; Problems, prospects and priorities, New Delhi: Inter-India Publications, 1997.

Seema Kazi: Report on Muslim Women in India, sponsored by Minority Rights Group International, 1999.

Usha Nayar et al.: An analytical study of education of Muslim women girls in India, Department of Women and Child Development, 2007.

11

Terrorism: A Threat to Human Rights Education

Rekha Trivedi

The human cost of terrorism has been felt in virtually every corner of the globe. The United Nations family has itself suffered tragic human loss as a result of violent terrorist acts. Terrorism has a very real and direct impact on human rights, with devastating consequences for the enjoyment of the right to life, liberty and physical integrity of victims. In addition to these individual costs, terrorism can destabilize Governments, undermine civil society, jeopardize peace and security, and threaten social and economic development. All of these have a real impact on the enjoyment of human rights. Security of the individual is a basic human right and the protection of individuals is accordingly, a fundamental obligation of Government. States, therefore, have an obligation to ensure the human rights of their nationals and others by taking positive measures to protect them against the threat of terrorist acts and bringing the perpetrators of such acts to justice.

The Nature of Human Rights

Human rights are universal values and legal guarantees that protect individuals and groups against actions and omissions primarily by State agents that interfere with fundamental freedoms, entitlements and human dignity. The full spectrum of human rights involves respect for, and protection and fulfilment of civil, cultural, economic, political and social rights as well as the right to development. Human rights are universal—in other words, they belong inherently to all human beings—and are interdependent and indivisible.

What is Terrorism?

Terrorism is commonly understood to refer to acts of violence that target civilians in the pursuit of political or ideological aims. In legal terms, although the international community has yet to adopt a comprehensive definition of terrorism, existing declarations, and resolutions and universal "sectoral" treaties relating to specific aspects of it, define certain acts and core elements. In 1994, the General Assembly's Declaration on Measures to Eliminate International Terrorism, set out in its resolution 49/60, stated that terrorism includes "criminal acts intended or calculated to provoke a state of terror in the general public, a group of persons or particular persons for political purposes" and that such acts "are in any circumstances unjustifiable, whatever the considerations of a political, philosophical, ideological, racial, ethnic, religious or other nature that may be invoked to justify them."

Counter Terrorism measures

In recent years, however, the measures adopted by States to counter terrorism have themselves often posed serious challenges to human rights and the rule of law. Some States have engaged in torture and other ill-treatment to counter terrorism, while the legal and practical safeguards available to prevent torture, such as regular and independent monitoring of detention centres, have often been disregarded. Other States have returned the persons suspected of engaging in terrorist activities to countries where they face a real risk of torture or other serious human rights abuse, thereby violating the international legal obligation of non-refoulement.

Repressive measures have been used to stifle the voices of human rights defenders, journalists, minorities, indigenous groups and civil society. These practices, particularly when taken together, have a corrosive effect on the rule of law, good governance and human rights. They are also counterproductive to national and international efforts to combat terrorism. Respect for human rights and the rule of law must be the bedrock of the global fight against terrorism.

The Impact of Terrorism on Human Rights

Terrorism aims at the very destruction of human rights, democracy and the rule of law. It attacks the values that lie at the heart of the Charter of the United Nations and other international instruments: respect for human rights; the rule of law; rules governing armed conflict and the protection of civilians; tolerance among peoples and nations; and the peaceful resolution of conflict. Terrorist acts can destabilize governments, undermine civil society, jeopardize peace and security, threaten social and economic development, and may especially negatively affect certain groups. The destructive impact of terrorism on human rights and security has been recognized at the highest level of the United Nations, notably by the Security Council, the General Assembly, the former Commission on Human Rights and the new Human Rights Council. Specifically, Member States have set out that terrorism:

- Threatens the dignity and security of human beings everywhere, endangers or takes innocent lives, creates an environment that destroys the freedom from fear of the people, jeopardizes fundamental freedoms, and aims at the destruction of human rights;
- Has an adverse effect on the establishment of the rule of law, undermines pluralistic civil society, aims at the destruction of the democratic bases of society, and destabilizes legitimately constituted governments;
- Has adverse consequences for the economic and social development of States, jeopardizes friendly relations among States, and has a pernicious impact on relations of cooperation among States, including cooperation for development; and
- Threatens the territorial integrity and security of States, constitutes a grave violation of the purpose and principles of the United Nations.

International and regional human rights law makes clear that States have both a right and a duty to protect individuals under their jurisdiction from terrorist attacks. The right to life, which is protected under international and regional human rights treaties, such as the International Covenant on Civil and Political Rights, has been described as "the supreme right" because without its effective guarantee, all other human rights would be without meaning. As such, there is an obligation on the part of the State to protect the right to life of every person within its territory. It is important to highlight the obligation on States to ensure the personal security of individuals under their jurisdiction where a threat is known or suspected to exist. This, of course, includes terrorist threats. In order to fulfil their obligations under human rights law to protect the life and security of individuals under their jurisdiction, States have a right and a duty to take effective counter-terrorism measures, to prevent and deter future terrorist attacks and to prosecute those that are responsible for carrying out such acts.

Terrorism and International Humanitarian Law

International humanitarian law contains a set of rules on the protection of persons in "armed conflict", as that term is understood in the relevant treaties, as well as on the conduct of hostilities. These rules are reflected in a number of treaties, including the four Geneva Conventions and their two Additional Protocols, as well as a number of other international instruments aimed at reducing human suffering in armed conflict. Many of their provisions are now also recognized as customary international law.

There is no explicit definition of "terrorism" as such in international humanitarian law. However, international humanitarian law prohibits many acts committed in armed conflict which would be considered terrorist acts if they were committed in times of peace.

Acts of terrorism which are committed outside of armed conflict generally constitute crimes under domestic and, depending on the circumstances, international criminal law that should be regulated through the enforcement of domestic and international criminal law.

The Promotion and Protection of Human Rights and Countering Terrorism

As terrorism impacts on human rights and the functioning of society, measures can be adopted by States to counter terrorism. As mentioned above, because terrorism has a serious impact on a range of fundamental human rights, States have not only a right but a duty to take effective counter-terrorism measures. Effective protection measures for terrorism and the protection of human rights are complementary and mutually reinforcing objectives which must be pursued together as part of States' duty to protect individuals within their jurisdiction.

The international community is committed to adopting measures that ensure respect for human rights for all and the rule of law as the fundamental basis of the fight against terrorism, through the adoption of the United Nations Global Counter-Terrorism Strategy by the General Assembly in its resolution 60/288. Member States have resolved to take measures aimed at addressing the conditions conducive to the spread of terrorism, including lack of rule of law and violations of human rights, and ensure that any measures taken to counter terrorism comply with their obligations under international law, in particular human rights law, refugee law and international humanitarian law.

The promotion and protection of human rights along with countering terrorism is an obligation of States and an integral part of the fight against terrorism. National counter terrorism strategies should, above all, seek to prevent acts of terrorism, prosecute those responsible for such criminal acts, and promote and protect human rights and the rule of law. At the outset, it is important to highlight that the vast majority of counter terrorism measures are adopted on the basis of ordinary legislation. In a limited set of exceptional national circumstances, some restrictions on the enjoyment of certain human rights may be permissible. Ensuring both the promotion and protection of human rights and effective counter-terrorism measures, nonetheless, raises serious practical challenges for States. One such example is the dilemma faced by States in protecting intelligence sources, which may require limiting the disclosure of evidence at hearings related to terrorism, while at the same time respecting the right to a fair trial and the right to a fair hearing for the individual. These challenges are not insurmountable. States can effectively meet their obligations under international law by using the flexibilities built into the international human rights law framework. Human rights law allows for limitations on certain rights and, in a very limited set of exceptional circumstances, for derogations from certain human rights provisions. These restrictions are specifically conceived to provide States with the necessary flexibility to deal with exceptional circumstances, while at the same time—provided a number of conditions are fulfilled—complying with their obligations under international human rights law.

INDIAN PERSPECTIVE ON TERRORISM

A common definition of terrorism is the systematic use or threatened use of violence to intimidate a population or government for political, religious, or ideological goals. Terrorism in India, according to the Home Ministry, poses a significant threat to the people of India. Terrorism found in India includes ethno-nationalist terrorism, religious terrorism, left wing terrorism and narco terrorism. People who are disgruntled and who are unable to get their desires fulfilled by normal and accepted methods in society are resorting to terrorism. Some other causes for which terrorism is resorted to, may be genuine, like a protest from people to come out of bondage or fight for freedom. Even such causes do not support terrorism, when there are other channels and methods to solve the problem.

Terrorism in India is not new, but it has increased very rapidly in the last few years. Terrorism in India should be looked upon as an integral part of our colonial legacy. The British followed the policy of 'divide and rule' and ultimately divided the subcontinent into two nations, which later grew into three after the independence of Bangladesh. Post-independence and post-partition violence and terrorism were unprecedented. This partition on the basis of religion, faith and community has sown seeds of hatred, violence, terrorism, separatism and communal divide and is predicted to be growing and flowering for a long time by the experts of international relations.

Terrorism is a global problem and as such, it cannot be solved in isolation. What is needed ultimately is—international co-operative efforts to fight against this global menace. All the governments of the world should simultaneously and continuously crack down on militants and terrorists. The global menace can be reduced and eliminated only by close co-operation between various countries. The countries from where militancy springs should be clearly identified and declared as terrorist states. It is very difficult for any terrorist activity to thrive for long in a country unless there is strong external support to it. Terrorism achieves nothing, solves nothing and the quicker this is understood, the better.

It is sheer madness and an exercise in futility. In terrorism, there cannot be a victor or vanquished. If terrorism becomes a way of life, the leaders and heads of states are usually blamed. It is a common consensus that this vicious circle is their own creation and only their combined and pooled efforts can check it. Terrorism is a crime against humanity and should be dealt with an iron hand and the forces behind it should be exposed. Terrorism adversely affects the quality of life and hardens attitudes.

The danger is clear and present in front of India and there is no denying of the fact that major terror organizations like ISIS and Al Qaeda with deep pockets are now turning their attention towards India. Given the scenario that is building up, it is extremely important for India to thoroughly revamp its internal security architecture and make it prepared for the worst of the eventualities. The Syrian example is right in front of India as to what happens when terrorism is not nipped in the bud. India's state level law enforcement agencies are in dire strate. Be it the incident of 26/11 or that of the sheer ignorance and failure of the Bengal Police to prevent the massive growth of Jamaat terror network, vindicate that much is left to be desired from the state level agencies who still depend much on the central agencies during critical situations, be it for the 26/11 kind of terror, the dependence on NSG or for the Bengal terror network investigation, the indispensability of NIA. Thus, there is not just a need to comprehensively improve, upgrade and sensitize the state level law enforcement, intelligence, investigation and counter terror organizations but also to have a new and comprehensive approach towards creation of a National Critical Infrastructure Protection Policy for protection of India's critical infrastructure.

Terrorism is not confined to any area or activity. It is finding its place in the elections conducted in our country to elect members to legislatures and parliament. Many a times, instances have the candidates are shown taking the help of terrorists to win their elections. As long as violence pays dividends much more easily and is allowed to go unchecked, the animal in man favours its use instead of peaceful methods. This is human nature.

Governments, all over the world are doing their best to put an end to terrorism. There are a few who encourage and support terrorism in other countries to meet their own political ends. The U.N.O. also is unable to completely eliminate this evil, even though it is able to contain it. But use of violence to check violence cannot be solution in the long run.

The only remedy to this evil appears to be the diagnosis of the root cause for each act of terrorism and if there is a genuine reason behind it, it is better to concede the demand. If terrorism is based on issues which are immoral and not acceptable, the sure and powerful weapon against it appears to be non-violent "satyagraha" introduced by Mahatma Gandhi.

Conclusion

Terrorism can be seen as a virus in the world body. The U.S. and other nations are attempting to solve the terrorist problem by trying to eliminate all of its manifestations around the world. This is like trying to eliminate a virus by removing one cell at a time, while damage to the host body (the world), increases with each violent removal, and more illnesses (terrorists) are generated. Groups such as Al Qaeda are only effects, not causes.

The causes are desperate poverty, oppression, unemployment and a future without hope. Terrorist organizations often provide a distorted sense of meaning and purpose for disempowered people.

To deal effectively with terrorists, the U.S., together with other wealthy nations, needs to come into heartfelt dialogue with true representatives of those who are dispossessed and impoverished. The approach that can stop terrorism from multiplying lies in developing a long-term plan, supported and financed by all nations of the world, addresses the basic needs of all people on the planet, and helps them in an equitable, fair way. This will provide a new sense of hope, meaning and purpose for them, freeing them from the despair that leads to fundamentalism and terrorism. With a new horizon of hope, people's thoughts will naturally turn from death and destruction towards life and creation where 'love, peace and brotherhood' will be the main 'mantra'.

REFERENCES

Books

- Aggarwal, Dr. H.O. *Human Rights*, Central Law Publications, 13th edn (2011).
- Kapoor, Dr. S.K. *International Law and Human Rights*, Central Law Agency, 16th edn (2012).
- Robertson, A.H. and Merrills, J.S. *Human Rights in the World*, Universal Publishing Co. Pvt. Ltd. 1st edn (2005).

Websites

- www.oneindia.com/feature/terrorism-india-bangladeshpakistan-dangers-1555431.html
- www.souledout.org/healing/endterrorism/endterrorism.html
- Office of the United Nations High Commissioner for Human Rights, Terrorism and Counter-terrorism Fact Sheet No. 32.

12

Crime Against Women: A Threat to Human Rights

Raj Kumar

A crime against women is not a new phenomenon in Indian society but from few decades the dimensions of crime against women are changing rapidly. Most of us are well aware about the crimes against women such as murder, rape, sexual slavery, bride burning, domestic violence, dowry, sexual harassment, women trafficking, acid attacks, widow exploitation, kidnapping and abduction, molestation, etc. but some crime against women are emerging with new dimensions and require new tools to fight against them. Hardly a day passes without news regarding the emerging crime against women somewhere around us.

Crime may be defined as violation of law in a particular society or an evasion of rights and responsibilities imposed by the government in a particular state. Stephen describes it as an "act which is forbidden by law and revolting to the moral sentiments of society." Crime is mainly of two kinds—first: Crime against state and second: Crime against society.

To protect women from crime against them, several new legislations have been brought and amendments have also been made in existing laws in the context of handling these crime effectively. But, even after the availability of good and strong law, the crime against women are emerging with new shapes and complexities. Apart from it, public is demanding for new specific laws to handle the already existed and identified crime which have been emerging with new faces such as honour killings, acid attacks, brutal gang rapes, etc.

In the era of globalization and human rights, everyone is entitled to enjoy all human rights irrespective of their sexual orientation. The several nations of the world, even after rectifying the international instruments such as Universal Declarations and International Covenants, remained without weapons for combating the violation against women. To promote and protect women rights, on December 18, 1979, the General Assembly adopted the Convention on the Elimination of all forms of Discrimination Against Women (CEDAW). Although, it influenced the formulation and amendment of domestic legislative policies regarding every kind of discrimination against women. But the lacking International Human Rights law for addressing the emerging problems of violence against women was a big challenge before international community. To address the violence against women all over the world, the United Nations has appointed a Special *Rapporteur* on violence against women and itself has developed a Declaration on the Elimination of Violence Against Women, 1993. Violence against women is defined in the declaration as follows:

> Any act of gender based violence that results in, or is likely to result in, physical sexual or psychological harm to women, including threat of such acts, coercion or arbitrary deprivation of liberty, whether occurring in public or in private life.

Violence against women—particularly, intimate partner violence and sexual violence against women—are major public health problems and violations of women's human rights.

A total of 2,44,270 incidents of crime against women were reported in the country during the year 2012 as compared to 2,28,650 in the year 2011 recording an increase of 6.4% during the year 2012. These crimes have continuously increased during 2008-12 with 1,95,856 cases in the year 2008; 2,03,804 cases in 2009; 2,13,585 cases in 2010; 2,28,650 cases in 2011; and 2,44,270 cases in the year 2012.

In this chapter, the author has included crime that are rapidly emerging in Indian society and urgent specific measures are required to fight against them.

Acid Attack on Women

Acid attack violence is a premeditated form of assault involving the throwing, pouring, or administering of acid, or other similarly corrosive substance, on an individual, with the intention to seriously maim, disfigure, torture, or kill. The victims of acid violence are overwhelmingly women and children, and attackers often target the head and face in order to maim, disfigure and blind. The act rarely kills but causes severe physical, psychological and social scarring, and victims are often left with no legal recourse, limited access to medical or psychological assistance, and without the means to support themselves. There are an estimated 1,000 acid attacks per year in India.

The brutality of this crime can be felt and understood by reading only few heart rending and horrifying instances of acid attacks. Few instances related to acid attacks are given as follows:

Pratima Choudhary was attacked along with her sister Bhavna in Meerut in 2003. She was the sole bread earner of her family when the sisters were attacked by a 65-year old man whose advances Bhavna had rejected. While Bhavna sustained 52 per cent injuries, parts of Bhavna's hands were burned in the attack. Pratima is still undergoing treatment while Bhavna fends for her family by taking up odd stitching jobs.

In a case of Haseena Hussain (Bangalore), the Haseena's former employer Joseph Rodrigues attacked by throwing acid on her face and head because of her refusal to work for him. The accused, Rodrigues, had been pestering Haseena to work for him again after she left his failing company and began work in another firm. When Haseena refused to return, he poured a full jar of sulphuric acid over her, which resulted in severe disfigurement of her face and body and complete loss of sight. The acid burnt a hole in her head, dissolved her lips, nose and one of her earlobes, welded one side of her neck to her shoulder, transformed the shape and colour of her face, and left her blind in both eyes. Her fingers were also fused together.

It was an absolutely horrendous attack. Haseena has had to go through 18 surgeries costing six lakh rupees and still she is blind and has severe disfigurement. As a result, she has been unable to get employment and even though she requires more surgery, it has been indefinitely postponed due to financial constraints.

In 2005, Laxmi was attacked with acid by a spurned lover 17 years elder to her, while she was going to a bookstore. The deadly attack disfigured her face, ears, hands and chest. Laxmi, survivor of acid attacks, reveals about the brutality of the acid attacks. In her own words which have been stated to a news agency that life never remains the same after an acid attack.

Most of the victims come from poor families and don't have enough money to undergo plastic surgeries. The medications cost lakhs of rupees. Even after eight years, she has some surgeries left. It is a never-ending fight.

Judicial Response

Acid attack survivor Laxmi had filed a PIL in Supreme Court. Through the petition, she has demanded two things from the court. First, strong regulations on the sale of acid and second, harsher punishment for the acid attackers. Subsequently, the apex court on July 18 directed that the crime be made a non-bailable offence and ordered state governments to pay ₹ 3 lakh compensation to the victims. The court also asked states to frame rules to regulate the sale of acid. The ruling brought her some happiness, but attacks continue even after the ruling.

Joseph Rodrigues vs. State of Karnataka

Following a long drawn out five-year criminal trial in the Sessions Court, in which the victim was exhaustively cross examined, the accused was only convicted for causing grievous hurt and not attempted murder as the prosecution argued for. In an extremely insensitive and unjust decision, where the judge did not account for the severity of the attack or its consequences to Haseena's life and livelihood, the accused was sentenced to a mere five years and three months in jail with a fine of three lakh rupees.

On appeal to the High Court of Karnataka at Bangalore, the conviction of the accused for attempt to murder was granted and the accused was sentenced to life imprisonment and a further two lakh rupees were awarded to Haseena. The judge rightly acknowledged that "the consequence of pouring a large quantity of sulphuric acid on the head is likely to cause death must be known to him (the accused) or has to be inferred and as such in our view, the offence clearly falls under the category of attempt to murder" (Para 43, *Joseph Rodrigues* vs. *State of Karnataka*, Karnataka High Court).

The Supreme Court has also raised the compensation to victims to ₹ 3 lakh and directed that states should pay the victim ₹ 1 lakh within 15 days and the rest within two months of the assault, while pointing out that the current amount that ranges between ₹ 5,000 and ₹ 1.5 lakh is inadequate to meet the costs of treatment and rehabilitation.

Governmental Response to Acid Attacks

With reference to acid attacks in 2009, first time the Law Commission had prepared and submitted their report on acid attacks. After that Justice Verma Committee given their recommendation for making acid attack a specific offence and now the Supreme Court has given the directions to the state for regulating the sale of acid and also raise the compensation.

The Ministry has also recommended that a new Section 326A (hurt by acid attack) and the Section 326B (attempt to throw or administer acid) that deals with offenders who burn or disable a person or cause grievous hurt, be made punishable with imprisonment of 5-7 years. Fines collected shall be given to victims of acid attacks. The provision is expected to compensate the victim for mental and physical trauma as well as medical expenses.

In 2002, the Bangladesh Parliament adopted and enacted the 'Acid Control Act' and the 'Acid Crime Control Act'. So, there is an urgent need of specific law for controlling the crime of acid attack and India should also follow the same path.

Crime of Rape Against Women

Instances of rape are appearing at least daily in the Indian print media. It appears that the policymakers, administrators, criminologists, sociologists, doctors, psychologists are in dilemma regarding the emerging dimensions of rape as well as fixing of the problem. Legally speaking, rape is defined in the Indian Penal Code as follows:

Rape—A man is said to commit "rape" who, except in the cases hereinafter excepted, has sexual intercourse with a woman under circumstances failing under any of the six following descriptions: First: Against her will; Secondly: Without her consent; Thirdly: With her consent, when her consent has been obtained by putting her or any person in whom she is interested in fear of death or of hurt; Fourthly: With her consent, when the man knows that he is not her husband, and that her consent is given because she believes that he is another man to whom she is or believes herself to be lawfully married; Fifthly: With her consent, when, at the time of giving such consent, by reason of unsoundness of mind or intoxication or the administration by him personally or through another of any stupefying or unwholesome substance, she is unable to understand the nature and consequences of that to which she gives consent; Sixthly: With or without her consent, when she is under sixteen years of age; *Explanation*: Penetration is sufficient to constitute the sexual intercourse necessary to the offence of rape. *Exception*: Sexual intercourse by a man with his own wife, the wife not being under fifteen years of age, is not rape.

According to an article of S.L. Sharma published in *The Tribune* rape has emerged as "India's fastest growing crime". As per the figures recorded by the National Crime Records Bureau (NCRB), there is a steep rise in rape cases from 2,847 in 1971 to 24,206 in 2011. Observation of cases registered with the Mumbai Police in the last two years indicates that a majority involved accused who are uneducated. But media reports have been showing an emerging trend of incest as well as gang rapes all over the country in last few decades. The threat of rape confronts all females, old or young, beautiful or plain looking, rich or poor. Even nine months old females and eighty years old women have been subject to rape. The rapist can be any one from the victim's own father, brother, relative, colleague, neighbor, servant, policemen or soldier.

"Crime in India, 2012" report released by National Crime Record Bureau (NCRB) reveals that a decreasing trend in rape cases has been observed during 2008-09. Thereafter, an increasing trend in the incidence of rape has been observed during the periods 2009-12. These cases have reported a decline of 0.3% in the year 2009 over 2008, an increase of 3.6% in 2010 over 2009 and an increase of 9.2% in the year 2011 over the year 2010 and further increase of 3.0% in the year 2012 over 2011.

Madhya Pradesh has reported highest number of rape cases (3,425) accounting for 13.7% of total such cases reported in the country. Mizoram has reported the highest crime rate of 20.8 as compared to national average of 4.3.

According to the report of National Crime Record Bureau (NCRB), rape cases have been further categorized as incest rape and other rape cases.

Incest Rape

Incest refers sexual intercourse or enjoyment of sexual pleasure between two persons related to each other by consanguinity or affinity within degree that would render marriage invalid. Thus, it is clear that all the incest rapes are being committed by the near relatives who come under the degree of prohibited relationship and it is also said that incest rapes are committing against girls and women within the highest protected boundaries of their own homes.

A latest case of incest rape of 22 year old girl in lucknow reported on September 5, 2013 in a Hindi newspaper and according to the news, she was continuously being raped by her father and brother from last nine years. The detail of figure about incest rape cases are given as follows:

Scenario of Incest Rape in India

Incest rape cases have increased by 46.8% from 267 cases in 2011 to 392 cases in 2012 as compared to 3.0% increase in overall rape cases. Maharashtra (77 cases) has accounted for the highest (19.6%) of the total such cases reported in the country.

Most of the incest cases remained unreported due to the pressure of family members on the victims and the fear of bad publicity of her own family in the society.

Gang Rapes

"Gang rape is a global problem but prevalent most in India and South Africa." South Africa even has a term for recreational gang rape, "Jackrolling," with a 2010 study reporting 7 per cent of men participating in it for "fun". In America gang rapes shrouded in a culture of silence, while gang rapes in Cairo's Tahrir Square have taken the sheen off the Arab Spring.

In May 2012, a case of gang rape of law student of Bhagat Phool Singh Mahila University, Haryana committed. In this rape four youths were involved.

On December 16, 2012, Delhi gang rape incidence, in which a 23-year-old physiotherapy student was sexually assaulted and brutally injured in a moving private bus. She later died in a Singapore hospital during her treatment. Entire nation became shocked after this brutal incident of gang rape.

On August 22, 2013, five accused were involved in the brutal gang rape of a 22-year-old photo journalist in Mumbai. One of the accused Vijay Jadhav allegedly told the police that they have committed similar crime earlier on four rag-pickers at the same spot.

On September 21, 2013, a 19-year-old Dalit girl was allegedly gang raped in Sirsa District, Haryana by three boys from the dominant caste.

There are various heart-rending stories related to gang rape which cannot be articulated here. Although there is no authentic figure available regarding to gang rapes in India, yet the nature of maximum instances are horrifying.

National Crime Record Bureau does not collect data on gang rapes separately from rapes neither in the form of crime category nor in the numbers of gang rapes.

In the case of a rape and murder such as the December 16 Delhi case, the 'principle offence' is murder since it attracts a maximum penalty of death. As a result, rapes that end in murder are recorded only as murders in NCRB's statistics.

Incidence of Rape in India

Rape incidence during 2008-12 according to the report released by National Crime Record Bureau (NCRB), 2012 are as follows: (year: no of rape incidence) (2008: 21,467); (2009: 21,397); (2010: 22,172); (2011: 24,206); (2012: 24,923).

There were 24,915 victims of rape out of 24,923 reported rape cases in the country during the year 2012. 12.5% (3,125) of the total victims of rape were girls under 14 years of age, while 23.9% (5,957 victims) were teenage girls (14-18 years). 50.2% (12,511 victims) were women in the age-group 18-30 years. However, 12.8% (3,187 victims) victims were in the age-group of 30-50 years while 0.05% (135 victims) was over 50 years of age.

The report of National Crime Record Bureau, 2012, clearly reveals the linkage between the offenders and rape victims is mentioned here as follows: More shocking news is that offenders were known to the victims in as many as in 24,470 (98.2%) cases. Parents/close family members were involved in 1.6% (393 out of 24,470 cases) of these cases, neighbors were involved in 34.7% cases (8,484 out of 24,470 cases) and relatives were involved in 6.5% (1,585 out of 24,470 cases) cases.

Government Response to Crime of Rape

After the 16 December Delhi gang rape, the people from all over the country showed their anger and protest against the Central Government and demanded for law reforms. Consequently, Indian rape laws have been given new force by making them strict.

Judicial Response to Crime of Rape

Death penalty was awarded to the four convicts in December 16 gang rape and murder case by the fast track court on December 13, 2013. Accordingly, the convicts be hanged by neck till they are dead, "Additional Sessions Judge Yogesh Khanna said while pronouncing the verdict. 'The offence in the present case has been committed in an extremely brutal, grotesque, diabolical, revolting and thus dastardly manner so as to arouse intense and extreme indignation of society and has a grave impact of the crime on social order.'"

Civil Society Response

No doubt, the response of civil society regarding crimes against women is quite good but in the case of crime of similar nature that takes place against the women of dalit community or women from rural India, the response of civil society does not reflect in similar manner. When gang rape is committed against the woman of lower caste, no voice comes out from the society, no one comes out with Candle March procession and society. They bear it with pinpoint silence but, if it is committed in the metropolitan cities or against the girl belonging to upper caste, the protest and anger of the society as well as civil societies may be seen easily. Crime against any woman should be seen as a crime against all woman and it should not be seen as crimes against the women belonging to lower caste or crime against the women belonging to rural area.

Trafficking in Women

Trafficking in persons is a crime of the complex nature. Trafficking in persons is emerging as a business of huge profit for the criminals all over the world. Every year, thousands of men, women and children fall into the hands of traffickers, in their own countries and abroad. Traffickers in human beings make an estimated $32 billion annually in an illicit market that affects millions of victims worldwide every year. Almost every country in the world is affected by trafficking, whether as a country of origin, transit or destination for victims. In the past decade, the volume of human trafficking has grown to the extent that it is now the third largest form of transnational organized crime after firearms and drugs.

Women and children are vulnerable to trafficking. Some reasons such as commercial sexual exploitation, forced labour or services, slavery or practices similar to slavery, servitude or the removal of organs have been identified behind the trafficking of women through the different studies conducted at the national and international level. Global statistics on forms of exploitation show that trafficking in persons for purposes of sexual exploitation is more frequently detected than trafficking for forced labour. In India, the scale of commercial sexual exploitation and trafficking is steadily rising despite the existence of the Immoral Traffic (Prevention) Act, 1956.

Trafficking in women for sex work is an old problem, but the end of communism, the advent of governmental strategies of market autonomy and deregulation called neoliberalism, and the increasing inequality in wealth around the world has fueled a rapid growth in sex trafficking since the 1990s. More women than ever are being drawn into the most coercive segments of prostitution and many more are crossing national borders in order to do so. The increasing global inequality in wealth is driving this process, while ever tighter border regulations condemn more and more of these women to moving illegally.

Article 3, paragraph (a) of the Protocol to Prevent, Suppress and Punish Trafficking in Persons defines "Trafficking in Persons as the recruitment, transportation, transfer, harbouring or receipt of persons, by means of the threat or use of force or other forms of coercion, of abduction, of fraud, of deception, of the abuse of power or of a position of vulnerability or of the giving or receiving of payments or benefits to achieve the consent of a person having control over another person, for the purpose of exploitation. Exploitation shall include, at a minimum, the exploitation of the prostitution of others or other forms of sexual exploitation, forced labour or services, slavery or practices similar to slavery, servitude or the removal of organs".

Trafficking for the removal of organs may appear to be limited, as it accounts for less than 0.2 per cent of the total number of detected victims. India is a fertile country for the traffickers and it is being used by the traffickers as a centre of origin, transit and destination for trafficked persons.

In 2012, Global Report on Trafficking in Persons published by the United Nations Office on Drugs and Crime (UNODC), reported that between 2007 and 2010, women constituted the majority of victims of trafficking in persons detected globally. While the exact share of the total varies somewhat according to year, during the reporting period, between 55 and 60 per cent of the total number of detected victims were women.

The Fourth World Conference on Women in Beijing in 1995 often called the Beijing Conference, clearly named violence against women as a violation of human rights and fundamental freedoms.

Its final policy document, the platform for action, defined violence against women broadly in Sec. D, 114 as "any act of gender-based violence that results in, or is likely to result in, physical, sexual or psychological harm or suffering to women, including threats of such acts, coercion or arbitrary deprivation of liberty, whether occurring in public life.

The policy document on the Platform for action in Article 123 stated that the effective suppression of trafficking in women and girls for the sex trade is a matter of pressing international concern. Implementation of the 1949 Convention for the Suppression of the Trafficking in Persons and of the Exploitation of the Prostitution of Others as well as other relevant instruments, need to be reviewed and strengthened. The use of women in international prostitution and trafficking networks has become a major focus of organized international crime.

The Special Rapporteur of the Commission on Human Rights on violence against women (who has explored these act as an additional cause of the violation of the human rights and fundamental freedoms of women and girls) is invited to address, within her mandate and as a matter of urgency, the issue of international trafficking for the purposes of the sex trade, as well as the issues of forced prostitution, rape, sexual abuse and sex tourism. Women and girls who are victims of this international trade are at an increased risk of further violence, as well as (unwanted pregnancy) and sexually transmitted infection, including infection with HIV/AIDS.

Studies by various organizations have revealed that girls from poverty-stricken villages in Assam, West Bengal, Jharkhand, Bihar, Odisha and even from Uttar Pradesh, Madhya Pradesh and Andhra Pradesh are trafficked to Haryana, Punjab via Delhi for forced marriages.

Human Trafficking for Forced Marriage in India

On September 20, 2013, *The Hindu* published a report about the practice of trafficking for forced marriage in India. This report revealed a story about a trafficked girl whose name was Paro. She was trafficked from the West Bengal to Haryana.

According to Mr. Kant, "hundreds of girls and women like Paro are sold-off by human traffickers as brides in Haryana villages since the past several years. A skewed sex ratio (877 females per 1,000 males) in the State is the prime reason behind the mushrooming of such organized syndicates. As reported in the latest report by United Nations office on Drugs and Crime (UNODC), a field study by Drishti Stree Adhyan Prabodhan in 1992 Haryana village covering 10,000 household revealed that over 9,000 married women had been bought from other States. They are purchased brides as Paro from outside the State.

Honour Killing

On September 20, 2013, in an apparent case of 'honour' killing, an 18-year-old girl was burnt to death by her parents at Balakati, about 20 km from the Bhubaneswar, Odisha. The victim's parents, Shantilata and Radhagovind, were against their daughter's affair with Nigamananda, who was already married.

In another instance committed on September 18, 2013, the young couple Nidhi Barak and Dharmendra Barak was brutally burnt to death in full public view on Wednesday evening at Gharnavathi village of the Rohtak District in Haryana. Nidhi Barak was lynched by her own family, who also broke the limbs of 23-year-old Dharmendra Barak before beheading him and dumping his mutilated body in front of his house. Both had been in a relationship for almost three years.

Honour killing is not a new problem in our society but due to recent media attention it has attracted local as well as global attention of governmental and non-governmental human rights promotion and protection agencies. The problem of honour killing existed all over the world, including India.

Honor killings are a form of gender violence rooted in conceptions of family honor and shame. Family honor depends on the bravery and courage of men and the sexual modesty of their women. Failures by either men or women can inflict damage on the whole family. Thus, when a woman fails to behave modestly or engages in sex outside marriage, she brings humiliation and shame upon her entire family. Under some circumstances, family members react by killing her in order to preserve the honor of the family. Families that kill their daughters may find this painful and difficult, yet feel driven to do so in order to preserve their honor from the slurs and assaults of others. Killings occur not only when women chose to have sex outside marriage, but also when they are suspected of doing so, even when there is no basis for the suspicion.

The causes behind honour killing may be varied from place to place all over the world. In India, caste factor plays a dominant role in committing the incidence of honour killings. Few instances of honour killings are as follows:

In July 2009, Monika Dagar, 21, secretly married Gaurav Saini, 24, who belonged to a lower caste and would thus be unacceptable to her family and community. A week later, Dagar's relatives arrived at the place the couple was living, accompanied by the police, who arrested Saini on kidnapping charges, despite Dagar's protests. He was eventually released but was unable to trace his wife despite repeated appeals for police assistance. In October, Saini was informed that his wife had died of pneumonia; the circumstances were such that Saini believes that she was murdered by her family. The police did not investigate the cause of her death, and Saini has brought a case against them.

Another case in Tamil Nadu indirectly reflects the crime against women. In this case Abhirami belongs to the Kallar (OBC) caste and she has joined a Teacher's Training College in Varothandu, near her village, Surakotai in Tanjavur district, Tamil Nadu. On the bus to college, she met and befriended a young Dalit boy, Marimuthu. This was reported to her family who confined her to the house and tried to force her to marry her 35-years-old alcoholic maternal uncle. Abhirami contacted Marimuthu and they eloped. The helpless young couple went from place to place, and it was only after they met some Communist Party of India (Marxist) members that they could go to Kumbakonam and get married. That was on September 16, 2010. After the birth of their daughter, Soundaraya, the couple returned to village to live with Marimuthu's family. However, just before Soundaraya's first birthday, Marimuthu was contacted by Abhirami's brother on the pretext of gifting the child a gold chain. On May 25, 2012, Marimuthu left home to meet his brother-in-law. He did not return. The next morning, his body, hacked to pieces, was found near the river. Abhirami's father and brother surrendered to the police confessing to the murder.

There are numerous heart-rending stories related to honour killing that cannot be mentioned here. Although, there is no authentic figure available regarding to honour killing with reference to India but the available estimated current figures regarding honour killings are horrifying.

Civil Society Response to Honour Killing

The civil society response in this regard is not said to be good. Only handful NGOs are working towards eliminating the evil of 'honour killings' from the society.

An NGO Shakti Vani, has petitioned the apex court seeking action against such extra-judicial killings in the name of community honour as well as holding the member of Khaps accountable for such crimes.

All-India Democratic Women's Association (AIDWA) Haryana unit secretary Savita criticized the state and mainstream politics and said that the state, which had recorded dozens of such killings, had done nothing to curb this crime. AIDWA has also raised the demand for separate legislation against honour killings. Savita said that a memorandum with over one lakh signatures was submitted to the Union Law Minister a few months ago, along with a draft legislation.

Judicial Response to Honour Killing

Justifying capital punishment for honour killings, Justice Katju, who wrote the judgment for the bench, said it was time to stamp out these barbaric, feudal practices which are a blur on the nation. He also wrote that, "There is nothing honourable in honour killings and they are nothing but barbaric and brutal murders by bigoted persons with feudal minds".

The order came while upholding the conviction of a person who had killed his daughter in 2006 because she had left her husband and was living in an incestuous relationship with her uncle.

"If someone is not happy with the behavior of his daughter or other person, who is his relation or of his caste, the maximum he can do is to cut-off social relations with her/him, but he cannot take the law into his own hands by committing violence or giving threats of violence," the bench pointed out.

Earlier in 2011, the court had ruled that "honour killings" fell in the "rarest of rare" category and, as a deterrent, those including such crimes should be awarded the death penalty.

Thus, it can be said that honorable apex court of India is delivering the judgements of crime against women in the light of international human right law.

Conclusion

No doubt that the Government of India has initiated efforts to make new laws as well as to strengthen the laws already existed for curbing the crimes against women. Although, every crime on the basis of gender bias is a violation of human rights and it is also recognized by the global community during the Beijing Conference, 1995. The changing dimensions of the crime against women last few decades are eye-opener and posing a serious threat to the right to life of women. Emerging dimensions of the crime against women are reflecting the brutal face of our so-called civilized society. No doubt the law already exist for tackling the crime of rape but the same crime with new dimensions is emerging day by day in our country such as incest rapes and gang rapes. The government can provide protection to women and girls outside their homes in the case of rapes and gang rapes but how protection can be given in their own houses? Therefore, protection of women and girls from incest rape is a big challenge before the government as well as society. Emerging trend of incest rapes is also a serious threat to the concept of family as well as social fabrics. Some other crime such as acid attack and honour killing and trafficking in women are also big challenge before the society as well as government. There is an urgent need to tailoring new specific laws to tackle the crime of acid attack, honour killings, trafficking in women and girls. The Government of India has taken note for legal reforms regarding crimes against women. Just after Delhi gang rape, the Government of India formed a committee headed by Justice Verma. The committee has prepared a report which includes suggestions that have been received from public domain as well as from different institutions for the purpose of curbing the crime against the women and important suggestions submitted to the government. Author personally feels that there is an urgent need to explore all the possible dimensions and future trends of the crimes against women in advance through utilizing the multidisciplinary approach. A multidisciplinary research agenda should also be developed with the help of the experts of the different educational streams, expressly or impliedly related to the crime against women. The more emphasis should be given on the development of the preventive measures rather than measures related to the punishment after committing the crimes. Now, time has come when we cannot only believe in the statement which is always made by the experts of sociology, criminology and law that mindset of the people should be changed. Nobody speaks that how it can be changed. Therefore, apart from legal tool, there should be emphasis on developing new innovative tools for curbing crime against women. It may be possible by creating human rights culture in our society. The human rights culture in our society may only be created through disseminating human rights education to all without any discrimination. Only by doing so, the crime against women may be curbed.

REFERENCES

Dr. P. Batria, *Sex and Crime in India*, Uppal Publishing House, New Delhi, 1992, p. 11.

Dr. Devender Singh, Human Rights, Women and Law, Allahabad Law Agency, Faridabad. 2005, p. 40.

Article 1 of the Declaration on the Elimination of Violence against Women, A RES/48/104, 23, February, 1994, Available at http://daccess-dds-ny.un.org/doc/UNDOC/GEN/N94/095/ 05/PDF/N9409505.pdf?OpenElement, Accessed on September 8, 2013.

Violence against women, Intimate partner and sexual violence against women, Fact sheet No. 239, Available at http://www.who.int/mediacentre/factsheets/fs239/en/, Accessed on September 8, 2013.

Crimes in India, 2012, National Crime Record Bureau Ministry of Home Affairs, India, Available at http://ncrb.nic.in/CD-CII2012/cii-2012/Chapter%205.pdf, Accessed on September 8, 2013.

Mom Kunther and Irwin Loy, 'Acid Attacks Could Earn Life in Prison', The Phnom Penh Post, February 16, 2010; Cambodian League for the Promotion and Defense of Human Rights (LICADHO), 'Acid Attacks in Cambodia Continue to go Unchecked', January 29, 2010, available online at: http:// www.licadho cambodia.org/articles/20100129/105/index.html; James G. Gollogly, Say Bon Vath, Annika Malmberg, 'Acid Attacks in Cambodia: Serious Reminders of Personal Conflicts', *Asian Biomedicine*, Vol. 2, No. 4 (August 2008), pp. 329-34; Kate Wesson, 'A Situational Assessment Study of Acid Violence in Bangladesh', *Development in Practice*, Vol. 12, No. 1 (February 2002), pp. 96-100, as cited in Breaking the Silence: Addressing Acid Attacks in Cambodia, May 2010.

Acid Survivors Trust International, Available at http://www.acidviolence.org/, Accessed on September 8, 2013.

Acid Survivors Trust International, Available at http://www.acidviolence.org/index.php/news/india-supreme-court-orders-curb-on-sales-of-acid/, Accessed on September 8, 2013.

Nupur Sonar, 'Justice For Acid Attack Victims Should Be Compensative And Reparative', Tehelka.com, July 22, 2013, Available at http://www.tehelka.com/justice-for-acid-attack-victims-should-be-compensative-and-reparative/, Accessed on September 8, 2013.

HRLN, Available at, http://hrln.org/hrln/criminal-justice/pils-a-cases/62-joseph-rodrigues-vs-state-of-karnataka.html, Accessed on September 2, 2013.

I will continue to fight: Acid attack survivor Laxmi, Sunday, Jul 28, 2013, Agency DNA, Available at http://www.dnaindia.com/india/1866642/interview-i-will-continue-to-fight-acid-attack-survivor-laxmi, Accessed on September 2, 2013.

Available at, http://hrln.org/hrln/criminal-justice/pils-a-cases/62-joseph-rodrigues-vs-state-of-karnataka.html, Accessed on September 2, 2013.

Government Plan to Make Rape Law Gender Neutral, Himanshi Dhawan, *The Times of India*, Lucknow, Friday January 20, 2012, p. 6.

Article 375 of the Indian Penal Code, 1880.

The Big Story: Gang Rape, *India Today*, September 9, 2013, p. 29.

Dr. P. Batria, *Sex and Crime in India*, Uppal Publishing House, New Delhi, 1992, p. 15.

Chapter 5, Crime against Women, "Crime in India, 2012" Report published by the NCRB, New Delhi. Available at http://ncrb.nic.in/CD-CII2012/cii-2012/Chapter%205.pdf, Accessed on September 14, 2013.

Dr. P. Batria, *Sex and Crime in India*, Uppal Publishing House, New Delhi, 1992, p. 8.

Nabharat Times, New Delhi/Lucknow, September 5, 2013.

Law Student gang-raped; three held, Special Correspondent, Chandigarh, *The Hindu*, Allahabad, Sunday, May 20, 2012, p. 5.

Arti Dhar, Rape convicts may face a minimum of 20 years in jail, *The Hindu*, Wednesday, March 20, 2013, p. 10.

The Big Story: Gang Rape, *India Today*, September 9, 2013, p. 30.

Divya Trivedi, Dalit girl gang-rape in Haryana, *The Hindu*, Tuesday September 24, 2013, p. 3.

Rukmini S., India officially undercounts all crimes including rape, only the 'principle offence' in an FIR gets into NCRB data, *The Hindu*, Lucknow, Friday, September 13, 2013, p. 1.

Nirnimesh Kumar, Death for four gang rape convicts, 'court cannot turn a blind eye to sending a strong message to perpetrators of such crimes' *The Hindu*, Lucknow, Saturday, September 14, 2013, p. 1.

Human trafficking under spotlight at Conference of Parties meeting, Available at http://www.unodc.org/unodc/en/frontpage/2012/October/human-trafficking-under-spotlight-at conference-of-parties-meeting.html, Accessed on September 22, 2013.

United Nations Office on Drugs and Crimes, Available at http://www.unodc.org/unodc/en/human-trafficking/what-is-human-trafficking.html, Accessed on September 22, 2013.

Human Rights Law Network, Available at http://hrln.org/hrln/anti-trafficking.html, Accessed on September 2, 2013.

UNODC, Global Report on Trafficking in Persons 2012 (United Nations publication, Sales No. E.13.IV.1).

Sally Engle Merry, Gender Violence: A Cultural Perspective, Chapter 4, Gender Violence as a Human Rights Violation, Wiley-Blackwell, A. John Wiley & Sons. Ltd., Publication, p. 92.

Human Trafficking, Available at http://www.unodc.org/unodc/en/human-trafficking/what-is-human-trafficking.html, Accessed on September 22, 2013.

Fourth World Conference on Women, Proposals for Consideration in the Preparation of a Draft Declaration, Draft Plateform for Action, Available at http://www.un.org/esa/gopher-data/conf/fwcw/off/al-1.en, Accessed on September 23, 2013.

Devesh K. Pandey, "Raped, then sold off as a bride in a distand land, Hundreds of girls and women have been sold-off by human traffickers as brides in Haryana villages in the past several years", *The Hindu*, Lucknow, Friday, September 20, 2013, p. 2.

The Hindu, Lucknow, Saturday, September 21, 2013, p. 9.

Girl's parents, brother held for 'honour killings', with an eye on the vote bank, political parties continue to turn a blind eye to the

Khaps despite Supreme Court strictures, *The Hindu*, Lucknow, Friday, September 20, 2013, p. 3.

India: Prosecute Rampant 'Honor' Killings, Available at http://www.hrw.org/news/2010/07/16/india-prosecute-rampant-honor-killings, Accessed on July 14, 2013.

Killing Love with Violence and Politics, *The Hindu*, Lucknow. Friday, July 5, 2013, p. 9.

Honour killings: Supreme Court says those who kill for 'honour' deserve death sentence, Available at http://indiatoday.intoday.in/story/honour-killings-sc-for-death-sentence/1/137621.html, Accessed on September 22, 2013.

13

Media vis-à-vis Women: A Human Rights Perspective

Ram Kalap Tiwari

Violence against women is perhaps the most shameful human rights violation. It knows no boundaries of geography, culture or wealth. As long as it continues we cannot claim to be making real progress towards equality, development and peace.

Kofi Annan

Women safety in India has been of primary concern today. It is known fact that most women have been exploited at some point in time and most of them silently bear this humiliation. Nowadays, it has been impossible for women and girls to move freely without a constant worry. This issue is growing rapidly in Indian society. The incidents of exploitation and other violence have been discussed in this study.

Incidents

One of the most important challenges facing the modern Indian society is ensuring the safety of its citizens, particularly its women. The issue has become even more serious and crucial after the brutal gang-rape in Delhi on December 6, 2012, which was the last nail in the coffin and the latest anger of people came out in full fury. The incident is condemned nationwide and there are huge protests against this across the country (*India Today*). Media performed a tremendous role in reducing this type of incidents in the society.

ASSOCHAM (2012) in a survey found that 92% of working women felt insecure, especially during night, in all the major sectors. They have been demanding suitable security norms. The incidents of exploitation and crime against woman in 2011 was the highest in Delhi (NCRB report). The number of incidents was 24,270. Molestation percentage was 18.8%, sexual harassment 3.7%, rape 10.6%, cruelty by husband or relation 43.4%, kidnapping or abduction 15.6% or dowry deaths 3.8 pending in court are in range of 70 to 80 per cent (Report Ministry of Home Affairs, 2011).

NCRB report (2012) conforms that 30942 cases against women exploitation were reported. West Bengal reported 12.67% crimes against women. According to the 2013 NCRB statistics, West Bengal has topped in crime against women. The irony in the story is that the state is ruled by a woman CM.

The rapid increase in the cases of rape raised serious concern amongst activists, which is one of the most heinous crime and reflected society's attitudes towards women's body (Mukherjee, 2008). A recent incident took place in Delhi again on 15 January, 2014. This is an evidence of crime expansion.

Cruelty by husband and relatives continues to occupy the highest share (43.40%) among the crimes committed against women in 2011 followed by molestation (18.81%). 15.6% causes are that of kidnapping and abduction, 10.60% of rape, 3.80% of dowry deaths and 3.70% of sexual harassment (NSO, 2012).

The crimes against women in India are growing at a rapid speed. Women, irrespective of their class, caste and educational status are not safe from ancient period, even the culture of devdasi in temples, exploited women.

In the present century, India is fast growing and emerging as a global power but for half of its population, the women across the country, struggle to live life with dignity. Women are facing problems in every sphere of life whether it is employment, access to health care or property rights. They are discriminated by the society. In recent times, they are more victims of crime directed specifically at them, rape, kidnapping and abduction, dowry-relational crimes, or molestation, sexual harassment, eveteasing and many others. National statistics show that problems of unemployment, poverty, economic inequality gender discrimination, lack of proper education, prevail mostly in women, although they are the most important part of the society.

Government has banned gender discrimination and women have been guaranteed political equality with men, yet there is a difference between constitutional rights and rights enjoyed in reality by women (Bhuyan and Panigrahy, 2006). The Government of India has ushered in the new millennium by declaring the year 2011 as women's empowerment year to focus on a vision, where women are equal partners like men. Government policy has been to promote women's participation in political social and economic life of the national and identical access to health-care quality education, career and vocational guidance, employment, equal remuneration, occupational health and safety, social security and public office, etc. The objective has been also to strengthen legal systems aimed at elimination of all forms of discrimination against women and changing the societal attitudes and community practice by actual participation and involvement of both men and women.

With the passage of time, many movements have been advanced in relation to exploitation of women but still men are ahead in Indian society. According to Puranas, there was violence against women in ancient India but there was strong punishment for that offence irrespective of caste (Das, 1990). However, some main aspects of exploitation may be highlighted as: use of women to earn money, physical and mental harassment by men and family members in society, trafficking of women and violence against women.

Exploitation of women are various types and of different nature. It includes crimes involving sexual exploitation for economic gains like prostitution and trafficking, adultery, abduction, rape, wrongful confinement and murder, etc. Crimes related to women's property like dishonest misappropriation, breach of trust, domestic violence, dowry extortion and outraging the modesty of women, etc. are not only injurious and immoral for women but also for the society as a whole.

Rape in India is the most common crime against women (Kumar, 2008). Official sources show that rape cases in India have been double between 1990 and 2008. Some reflection of rape cases is presented in table below.

Table 1: Rape Victim and Accused Relationship 2012

S. No.	Accused Relationship	No. of Victim	Percentage of Victims
1.	Neighbors	207	29.32%
2.	Friends	200	28.32%
3.	Relatives	59	08.35%
4.	Employer/Coworker	17	02.41%
5.	Other Known person	197	27.90%
6.	Unknown stranger	26	03.68%
Total		**706**	**99.98%**

Source: Delhi Police (*The Hindu*, News Staff reported New Delhi, January, 19, 2013)

The above table shows that maximum of rape cases were committed by the known persons such as neighbors, friends, relatives and known persons. Only 3.68% cases were committed by unknown persons. It is clear from above figures that women are not safe even in their family and neighborhood.

Exploitation of women occurs in all societies, regardless of culture, region, religion, caste, group and economic status. The cause for exploitation against women is a complex combination of cultural, legal, economical and political factors. Yet it is generally accepted view that violence or exploitation of women is the result of patriarchal ideology, values and norms, unbalanced power relations, as well as strict division of labor, socialization processes, cultural customs and traditions. Poverty and low SES further exacerbate the problems.

The "Men's Action for Stopping Exploitation and Violence Against Women" (MASVAW), a community-based grassroots initiative and members-based network of male activists, focus on mobilizing men to end exploitation and violence against women, awareness-raising among youth, the public and local government, as well as advocacy with media and the government authorities, NGOs and universities. SAHAYOG, a non-profit organization promoting sustainable rural development in

Uttar Pradesh and Uttarakhand over the years evolved into an organization working on women's empowerment, women's rights and health issues.

Reason

There are some important reasons which allow such incidents to happen. One reason for increase in crime against women is ignorance of police participation. Nowadays, women have become more aware of their rights. Access to Mahila courts, legal and crime cells for women had also helped indirectly to encourage women to register their complaints. Media is playing positive and negative role in promoting such undesirable things on the screen of TV, cinema and advertisements. All these lead to increase atrocities against women. The low conviction rate of guilty is deplorable. Lack of evidence and guidance, loop holes in existing laws are some of the reasons for the rise in crime against women (Rana, 2004).

Constitutional and Legal Provisions

The principle of gender equality is enshrined in the Indian constitution in its preamble, fundamental rights, fundamental duties and directive principles. The Constitution of India not only grants equality to women but also empowers the state to adopt measures of positive discrimination in favor of women for neutralizing the cumulative socio-economic, education and political disadvantages faced by them. Articles 14, 15, 15(3), 16, 39(b), 39(c) and 42 of the constitution are of specific importance in this regard. Special initiatives for women include:

(i) National commission for women (1992)

(ii) Reservation for women in local self-government (1993)

(iii) National plan of action for the girl child (1991-2000)

(iv) National policy for the empowerment of women (2001) are very useful.

Role of Media

The sphere of influence of media is increasing day by day as the coverage of a small news article is very wide these days.

More importantly in a modern-knowledge society, media plays a role of facilitator of development, disseminator of information, and an agent of change. The present-day situation of our country demands an active and vibrant media. The frequency of incident is increasing these days. At the time of reporting of incidents, media should take care that no hatred is created among the sections of people. The Wardha Commission states that media, both print and electronic, had also to exercise restraint and screaming head lines should be avoided, it said "headlines in the case of rape of nun and murder of Christian boy and girl after rape has been noticed. One cannot imagine the damage that might have been caused to the polity by such headlines and reporting".

Media plays a very huge role in deciding the art and act of democracy. But, in general, every one of us has a feeling that the media is performing its responsibility properly in Indian democracy. It is indeed a very powerful tool. In ancient period, people tend to believe in the news which media delivers around the country. So, when something was published or telecast in media, one could infer the truth very easily. But conditions have changed erratically and dramatically.

The media can help in reducing the state of violence exploitation and crime in society, coverage of exploitation and violence against women began in full strength in recent years. Such coverage has led to social awareness, policy for protection of women and girls, expansion of service for female victim support and a rise in the media coverage on number of reported cases. Woody (2002) states that the media can be useful for providing responsible coverage of violence, exploitation and crime or sexual harassment and raise awareness of issues on high risk behaviors. It supports open dialogue within the community and family encouragement awareness and helps to offer services and information to victims. The media can also affect cultural standard on offences and incest in order to help victims confront the issue and to reduce stigma.

The media equally participates in disseminating public information on self-protection and safety strategies against exploitation, due to the impressive amount of individuals who rely on media for crime information. The media can therefore be highly efficient for certain types of openness. Media campaigns on prevention against these activities and information on the risks of involving in these acts, exemplify the means by which the media can have an important role in crime prevention.

The media can play a democratic role when it comes to the question of crime prevention. With more information being made public, the media educates the population on certain issues, which therefore encourage critical thinking on the part of the population and promotes responsibility on the part of the family and social institutions, agencies, organizations and governments. In this way, media has a key role to play in strengthening democracy.

The media's role in crime prevention may encourage proper policies as well as government initiative to allocate resources to local communities to implement prevention strategies. The media plays an active role in encouraging accountability of decision making which controls the design and implementation of public policies. The media can help to promote civic journalism, which fosters responsibility on the part of the media to provide reliable information and engage in positive crime prevention initiatives.

Suggestions

In my opinion, the following suggestions may be helpful in reducing the exploitation against Indian women in present social setup:

(i) Extensive police reforms
(ii) Security commission
(iii) Inspire public confidence
(iv) Legal protection of women
(v) Fast track court
(vi) Empowerment of women
(vii) Education program for women
(viii) Responsibilities of civil society
(ix) Media involvement.

Despite legal protection and many provisions for the development and betterment of women, the plight of women has still not improved. Discrimination and exploitation on the basis of gender constitutes a serious issue. The problem of women has achieved worldwide attention and several efforts have been made to bridge the seemingly ever-widening gap. Being all efforts to integrate women into the mainstream development procedure could not solve the problem (Deepa, 2012). Though, media, TV channels, newspapers and periodicals are filled with data pertaining to the problems of various incidents of exploitation against women, yet the picture shows no sign of improvement.

Dignity and well-being of women are important issues and no compromise under any circumstance can be done on that. It is the duty of the government to enact promptly with strict legal provisions to curb these activities. Strict and swift punishment should be given to those who are involved in these activities against women. Legal provisions should be implemented for the protection of women. Media should promote and give coverage to all these issues.

In the era of globalization, working women have become more vulnerable to intense exploitation: they are exposed to more and more risks and forced to ensure severe stress and strain, both physical and mental (*Times of India*, 2013).

There is need of social awakening as well as collective consciousness and change in the heart and attitudes of masses so that due respect and equal status is given to women. It is time when women need to be given their due share. This awakening can be brought by education compaigning among youth making them aware of existing social evils and the means to eradicate the same. Media can play an active role as it has reached every corner of the nation.

However, the representation of women in media has always been exploitative. It has, throughout the years, reduced women to nothing more that objects to be won, prizes to be shown off, and play things to be abused. It has also created a definition of beauty that women compare themselves to another work. Also, men compare the women in their lives to what they see on television screens, in magazines, both the self and society have suffered because of this assessment.

Kurosaki (2006) showed that women, when looking at photos of their bodies that were distorted as fat, cognitively processed the image in the same way as fearful information. The women were also shown true to life images of their body, displayed high brain activation pattern in the prefrontal context when viewing and interpreting body image, which illustrates that they process body image through emotions. Impulsive and emotional responses can elicit other negative mental and physical responses and prompt emotions such as depression.

Friederich et al. (2007) studied the impact of viewing images of fashion models. They found that anxiety ratings were "significantly higher" when the participants viewed images of idealized bodies. They found that the fear network of the brain is particularly activated when anxiety rating increases.

The sexual exploitation of women is especially predominant in advertising, which is impossible to escape because ads are omnipresent.

Bandura refers the concept of modeling. Through modeling, the observers learn what behaviors are appropriate in what situations and begin to set-up structure and rules for their environment based on the knowledge they obtained with their modeling. A great deal of information about human values, styles of thinking, behavior patterns and socio-structural opportunities and constraints is gained from modeled styles of behavior portrayed symbolically through the electronic media. The acceleration growth of electronic technologies has vastly expanded the range of models to which members of a society are exposed day in and day out (Bandura, 1995). He mentioned that the electronic media is a machine that quickly and efficiently structures new symbolic environments for human to construct and model. Women are indeed affected by ubiquitous, graphic and consequence-free depictions of ill-behaviors that surround women in all forms of the media.

Conclusion

Though, the status of women in India, both historical and social, has been one of respect and reverence, but even today, they are struggling for their own identity, shouting for diffusion of their voices and fighting for their own esteem. Despite the constitutional guarantee of equality, discrimination and exploitation of women in Indian society continue. It is high time now that women should get a respectable and identified position in the society. Awareness in the women as well as in society should be created and their equal rights should be effectively implemented by the Central and State Governments. Exploitation against women should be punishable. Media should play a positive role in presenting the facts of incidents against girls and women. In modern society changes have been taking place everywhere in almost every field but we are yet to protect honor of women.

In Indian modern society, it is essential that all women get education to live in a better world. Education will give them strength and societal status. It is essential that socio-economic empowerment for women must be ensured by the nation to reduce the exploitation which can help to improve the status of women.

REFERENCES

Bandura, A. (1999). "Social cognitive theory: An agentic perspective". *Asian Journal of Social Psychology*, 2, 21-41.

Crime against women (2011). National Crime Records Bureau (NCRB), Ministry of Home Affairs, India.

Crime in India (2012). NCRB Table 5.1, Ministry of Home Affairs, India, *India Today*, July 17, 2013.

Das, S. (1990). *Crime and Punishment in Ancient India*, Abhinav Publication, New Delhi.

Deepa, S. (2012). "Crime against women in India: A reality check". In Awadhesh Kumar and Jayanta Choudhary (eds), *Violence against Women and Children: Issues and Concerns*. Serials publication, New Delhi.

Friedric, H.C., Uher, R., Brook, S.S., Campbell, C. (2007). "I" am not as slim as that girl: Neural bases of body shape self-comparison to media images, *Neuro Image*, 3:7: 674-81.

India Today, January, 21, 2013.

Kurosaki, M., Shirao, N., Yama Waki, S. (2006). Distorted images of one's own body activates the prefrontal context in Young women: A functional magnetic resonance imaging study Biological Psychology, 25, 380-86.

Rama, A. (2004). "Violence against women", *International Journal of Ideas*, 23-24, India.

Times of India, July 26, 2013, p. 2.

Woody, J.D. (2002). Media coverage of child sexual abuse: An opportunity for family therapists to help families and communities, 30, 417-26.

14

Revisiting Human Rights in the Light of Future Threats

S.R. Verma

Human brain is a fascinating, evolutionary creation. It is with the help of this brain that man has been able to develop culture and civilization. Today, every thinking person feels an intense yearning for harmony and peace in every corner of the globe. Despite that, the world is threatened by various forms of violence such as nuclear war, chemical and biological warfare, terrorism, etc. Recent world events have created tremendous anxiety, fear and unrest in our lives.

In spite of the creation of world organizations such as United Nation Organization (UNO) with its various branches, many big and small wars, battles between nations have been and are being fought continuously. There have also been continuous conflicts, private and state terrorism and violence on account of issues related to religion, caste, class, sect, ethnicity and so on. This is the right time to revisit Human Rights in the light of future threats.

On 10th December, 1948, the United Nations General Assembly adopted and proclaimed the "Universal Declaration of Human Rights". The General Assembly proclaims this Universal Declaration of Human Rights as a common standard of achievement for all people and all nations, to the end that every individual and every organ of society, keeping this Declaration constantly in mind, shall strive by teaching and education to promote respect for these rights and freedoms and by progressive measures, national and international, to secure their universal and effective recognition and observance, among the people of territories under jurisdiction. United Nations General Assembly called upon all member states to adopt and implement these rights in their respective countries. Since then every 10th December is celebrated as the 'Human Right Day' all over the world. The World Conference of Human Rights (1993) said, "The Universal Nature of Human Rights and freedoms is beyond question." The Universal Declaration of Human Rights contains thirty (30) articles which can be grouped under five broad categories such as (i) Civil Rights, (ii) Political Rights, (iii) Economic Rights, (iv) Social Rights and (v) Cultural Rights. Here I would like to quote Executive Director of the New York based International League for Human Right Mr. Charles H. Norchi. He said, "In the final analysis, Human Right is really about human dignity—a notion familiar to India's civilization continues before West ever born."

National Human Rights Commission (NHRC) India

The concept of Human Rights is not new to India. It has been part of our civilization and cultural history for over five thousand years.

The National Human Rights Commission of India is an autonomous and statutory organisation. It has been created by an Act of Parliament. It was established on 12th October, 1993 under the Protection of Human Rights Act (PHRA), 1993 as amended by the Protection of Human Rights Amendment Act, 2006. It has a wide mandate and an array of functions catering to all sections. It has the powers of a civil court trying a suit under the code of civil procedure, 1908, for summoning and enforcing the attendance of witness and examining them on oath; discovery and production of any document; receiving evidence on affidavits; requisitioning any public record or copy thereof from any court of office and issuing commissions for the examinations of witnesses or documents etc.

The concept of Human Rights centres on truth and justice. These are 'Natural Rights'. Every man and woman has a natural claim on them by virtue of being a human being. These are sometimes called fundamental or basic Rights. The present human civilization is facing a crisis of survival. Peace in the life of human, society and nation appears to be threatened.

The possible sources of future threats may be the following:

1. Misuse of Technology
2. Misinterpretation of Religion
3. Human behaviour and Consumerism.

We have just entered the fifteenth year of the new millennium and war and terrorism are becoming the norm to resolve international conflicts. All the experience of bloody wars of the previous century and the wisdom thereby gained seems to have been wasted.

The cold war had ended but powerful nuclear states have not stopped war. The increasing militarization of science has now clearly threatened life and liberty of civil society, and endangers well-being of future generation.

It is not that conflicts or war did not exist at all in premodern societies. But the scale of human tragedy was smaller than today. There, the need for the quest for peace and non-violence has become extremely urgent and imperative now. It is very essential that we study and propagate the wisdom which will extricate mankind from this problem and which will save human civilization from self-destruction. It is in this context that the present paper seeks to discuss the relevance of Russell-Einstein Appeal of 1955.

Bertrand Russell was a prolific author on a rainbow of subjects. He for all his enthusiasm for science, does not agree that science is inherently a good thing rather for him science was something to be used and abused. It can be put to the service of good or evil. The power of the atom held a vast potential—as a reservoir of energy that could be harnessed for a wealth of benefits to mankind or as weapon of destruction on a scale previously unimaginable. As with any advanced science, atomic energy posed a choice for the human race for good and for ill.

A German born, theoretical physicist, originator of the Theory of Relativity, Albert Einstein advised president of America to build Atom Bomb. But, after Second World War

Einstein was strongest opponent of nuclear war. Einstein's thoughts went beyond the frontiers of science. He was a symbol of the struggle for peace and social justice. In 1955, a few weeks before he died, Einstein with Bertrand Russell issued a warning to the world leaders in The Russell-Einstein Manifesto against The Risk of Universal Death. The manifesto was signed by many Noble Laureates and was issued in London, 9th July, 1955. They invited the congress, and through it the scientists of the world and the general public to subscribed to the following resolution:

In view of the fact that in any future world war nuclear weapons will certainly be employed, and that such weapons threaten the continued existence of mankind, we urge the government of the world to realize, and to acknowledge publicly, that their purpose cannot be furthered by a World War, and we urge them consequently, to find peaceful means for the settlement of all matters of dispute between them.

This Russell-Einstein Manifesto was issued in London, 9th July, 1955 but it is very much relevant even today. Peace cannot be kept by force. It can only be achieved by understanding.

This is high time to get rid of all nuclear weapons everywhere. Therefore we demand that:

1. All nuclear weapons would be taken at once off "Alert" status.
2. All nuclear States start to negotiate, sign and ratify an effective treaty abolishing all mass destruction weapons.
3. Ban on the development and production of space weapons may be too ambitious right now.

The only reasonable approach to this problem is that disarmament measures must take place within a series of transparent, verifiable, parallel steps. This process must occur in tandem with nonproliferation measures. Nuclear Weapons serve no constructive purpose in the world.

Bertrand Russell and Einstein can prove true if government and the society at large assist us in tackling the problem of misuse of science and technology. We must encourage the teaching of ethics in scientific education. This will strengthen ethical awareness of the individual scientists and scientific community. This will also help to increase ethical awareness within the community and break down the public fears about the future. There is reason, what I think, gets divorced from the human heart, and leads to things like weapons of mass destruction and some of the other horrors of modern technology. But the human brain, which has created these weapons, is capable of overcoming them. Let us have the wisdom to put our common humanity above everything that divides us.

Vienna Declaration on Human Rights (1993) was a watershed in the history of Human Rights regime. Over the last two decades, the UN Commission on Human Rights is reflecting regularly on expanding boundaries of Human Rights regime. The current movement to bring 'Human Rights' to the centre stage of socio-political discourse provides an opportunity to revisit Human Rights in the light of future threats.

In spite of the monumental achievements of science, the dark side of science is that it also has the potential to demolish humanity from mother earth in the form of nuclear, chemical, biological and other hi-tech bombs, all products of science. The fanatic and misguided section of society misuses these very sophisticated weapons for annihilating precious and innocent human lives as well as other life forms.

We are a people composed of many races, many languages, many religious traditions, many political parties and many cultures. We are poor and rich, women and men, young and old. It is the diversity that indicates high degrees of interaction and integration for all communities.

In our Indian society, women have been given a remarkable position. They are considered Durga and Laxmi in Indian families. Ironically, these so-called Goddesses have to struggle hard for their survival. The society that worships girls during *Navratri* for *Kanya Pujan*, never hesitates while burning, molesting, beating and oppressing the girls. This dual perspective should change. The exploitation of others' rights does not always means physical suppression but the mental and psychological subjugation of any community, class and gender also come in the violation of human rights.

There is not just violence against women, there is violence against senior citizens and children as well. All this happens because there is imbalance in development of mind and heart. Our education has stuffed us with information and facts, but has made us dry and devoid of sensitivity. In life, we need two things, sensibility and sensitivity. Sensibility is of the intellect and a lot has been done in developing that. But not much has been to make people sensitive.

We need the perfect balance, only then there can be harmony. The mind always wants something new, but heart wants something old. You never say, "This is my new friend." You always say, "This is my old friend." Is not it? An old friendship is honoured. Education and environment at home and workplace should bring about change and awareness.

We are all aware that although recent advancement in science and technology have brought tremendous benefits to humanity, they have also increasingly raised ethical concerns. Ethical values have not been able to keep pace with the explosive development of science and technology. This trend is a serious threat to humanity. Thus, there is an important need to generate ethical guidelines in our scientific research especially in the fields of nuclear technology and biotechnology.

The call for values is currently echoing throughout every land, as educators and parents. More and more children are increasingly concerned about and are affected by violence, growing social problems and lack of respect for each other. Educators are, therefore once again being asked to address problems which have arisen within their societies. The knowledge should not be based on commercial interests only but it should teach the art of living. There is need to imbibe moral education from the very childhood.

It is not sufficient to simply pass the examination but one should inculcate the qualities of brotherhood and sympathy. Real knowledge makes us complete mentally, physically and spiritually and inspires us to imbibe the values in our life. If values are adopted, all the quarrels and difficulties in life would come to an end, enabling us to lead a life of peace and bliss. An educational programme should provide guiding principles and tools for the development of the complete person, recognizing that the individual comprises physical, intellectual, emotional and spiritual dimensions.

The next question that comes up is why modern science with all its advantages now poses a threat to the very survival of man and his environment? I will fail in my duties if I do not talk about Kedarnath disaster and environment protection. Environment is a subject which concerns all of us. Due to rapid urbanization and industrialization during last five decades, the environmental problems are fast increasing and India is no exception. Kedarnath disaster is the result of misuse of science and technology and human activity which has created an imbalance in ecology in Himalayan region.

Unchecked human activities and global climate changes will result in deficiency of water, food and land to live on the basic sources. All environmental pollution and problems lie in the fact that we all in general and scientists in particular, have divorced science and technology from ethics, moral values and Vedic teaching, the consequence of which we are experiencing today. Tribal people of Jharkhand (India) once said, that they are not frightened of snakes, but of educated people of the cities.

A Vedic outlook helps in keeping our greed for materials and resources in check. Sustainable development can only take place when we use the resources for our needs and not for our greed. In Vedic time we worshipped mountains, rivers, animals, and we believed that whole creation was divine and adored everything as God-given. Upliftment of human beings from animality to divinity was the aim of Vedic civilization. Unity in diversity was the recognized ideal of the Vedas.

With greater awakening among our people, the social, spiritual and legal obligations and availability of know-how from our ancient literature and our indigenous experiences and researches, a stage of take-off has been reached. With greater concern in the government and in the community for a cleaner and better environment, we would be able to force the industries to install appropriate effluent treatment plants and keep our environment clean.

Now, it is time to assess and evaluate various environmental problems and issues that mankind is facing. It is the time to propose a proactive action plan in order to save mother earth from further environmental degradation. Yes, collectively we can do it.

The Vedas and allied ancient literature forms the basic concept of environmental protection. Some of them are outlined here:

1. The five elements (Panch Bhutas) Akasha, Vayu, Agni, Aapah and Prithivi are the base of the environment.
2. The Vedas tell man that he is an inseparable part of all that exists.
3. Man as a symbol of the Earth, each of his indriyas representing a bhuta.
4. Each natural force is prescribed as Devta.
5. Respect nature and its components and use natural resources most economically.
6. Realize the interconnectedness of all that exists—the web of life.
7. Love all Nature as part of one's own being.
8. We must revisit present lifestyle in the current scenario.
9. There must be universal understanding on the environmental issue.
10. There should be global shift to a clean and green economy.
11. And last but not the least, save Mother Earth for generations to come.

In order to avoid misuse of science and technology we must encourage the teaching of ethics in scientific education.

All educational institutes must promote ethic courses in all fields of science and technology.

REFERENCES

Harry Dhand, Tea*ching Human Rights.*

Kalki, The Future of C*ivilization, 1948.*

Nagendra Si*ngh, Enforcement of Human* Rights.

Storey, David, *Vision of an Interfaith Future*, 1994.

"What went wrong? Western Impact and Middle Eastern Response", Oxford University Press, 2002.

15

A Sentinel of Cultural Diversity of Primitive Tribes: Sitakant Mahapatra

Madhu D. Singh and *Sweta Tomar*

Cultural diversity is the quality of diverse or different cultures, as opposed to monoculture or a homogenization of culture which leads to cultural decay. In fact, it can be said that cultural diversity is analogous to biodiversity. Just as biodiversity is essential for the longtime survival of life on earth, cultural diversity is equally vital for the longtime survival of humanity. That's why UNESCO in its Universal Declaration on Cultural Diversity calls it 'the common heritage of humanity'. It also states that the defence of cultural rights is an ethical imperative, inseparable from respect for human dignity. However, with the advent of globalization, advancement of technology and rapid urbanization, cultural diversity is under threat of getting homogenized. In such a scenario, the efforts of international bodies like UNESCO to preserve cultural diversity are indeed important.

One of the ways to preserve the cultural diversity of a society is to document its oral literature in written form. Renowned scholars around the world are engaged in the task of documenting various aspects of the culture of indigenous tribes. Among these sentinels of cultural diversity, Sitakant Mahapatra's name shines like a luminous star. A Jnanpith Award Winner and a highly distinguished administrative officer, he has rendered yeoman's service in preserving the cultural diversity of the primitive tribes of India by translating the folk songs of the tribes of eastern India. His anthology of Oral Poetry of the Primitive tribes of India, titled *They Sing Life* has been published by UNESCO Publishing under UNESCO collection of Representative Works.

Taking an overview of the efforts of international scholars to document the oral literature of the indigenous tribes in different parts of the world, the present paper, besides highlighting Mahapatra's contribution in preserving the cultural diversity of the primitive tribes of eastern India, would also critically analyse his views on maintaining a fine balance between development and cultural diversity.

There have been attempts world over to document the lifestyles of different primitive societies. As Mahapatra notes in the introductory remarks to his anthology *They Sing Life:* "On the American Indians there have been many learned books dealing with their poetry and songs. Jerome Rothenberg's *Technicians of the Sacred* and '*Shaking the Pumpkin* are two of the best representative collections on the subject. There is also Tedlock's *Finding the Centre: Narrative Poetry of the Zumi Indians*. There is of course that very valuable work of C.M. Bowra *Primitive Songs*."

So far as documentation of the cultural practices of tribals in India is concerned, during the British rule in India, the general approach of the administration towards the tribals, notes Mahapatra, was that of "non interference with their traditional lifestyles, customs and manners with a high degree of indifference towards the knowledge, and understanding of these systems. These communities were supposed to be too different, too exotic and difficult and there was no attempt to study, document and analyze their social pattern, lifestyles, value systems, performing or plastic arts, land use or land inheritance patterns, legal systems, etc." (*They Sing Life,* 15). However, there were some exceptions also. An English IAS officer W.G. Archer who worked as deputy commissioner in Southern Bihar did compile and translate some of the song poems of the Mundas and Oraons of that area under the title *The Blue Grove* and *The Dove and the Leopard*. Verrier Elwin also compiled and translated quite a large corpus of the song poems of the tribes of Middle India. In the post independence India, contribution of scholars like Mahapatra in this field is undoubtedly remarkable.

As in the rest of the world, in India too, cultural diversity is under severe threat. The erosion of traditional cultural forms, according to Mahapatra, springs from the interface of rapid economic growth, technological changes, new patterns of production, endless consumerism, increasing market forces and global tourism. Each of this has a possible unsettling impact on traditional value systems and cultures.

An avid lover of the cultures of the primitive tribes, Mahapatra has been intensely conscious of the need of documenting the rich cultural heritage of the tribes. He writes:

> The fascinating tribal way of life in different regions of the country constitutes a valuable treasure of our heritage. For a long time we took it for granted that they were with us anyway as living traditions and as such there is no serious need to document them. Living forms no doubt they are, but slowly we are realizing that they are not insulated from the forces of change and modernization. In the process of socio-economic change, the forms get either modified, distorted and damaged. These are inevitable results of rapid change. The adjustments for survival sometimes affects their core image, the original motif and authenticity of the cultural profiles. At other times they even suffer dissolution and death. Hence the urgency of such documentation. (*Hinterland of Creativity*, 160)

Mahapatra's interest in the tribal art forms motivated him to document the oral poetry of the tribes of eastern India, and it has remained a passion with him ever since. It took him to numerous villages of eastern India where he stayed for long periods during a two year Homi Bhabha Fellowship (1975-77) Way back in 68-69, he learnt one of the major tribal languages of the region, Santhali, knowing which he could access the other four allied and sister languages. This enabled him to have the privilege of being taken into confidence and living in their village over a two year period and returning there now and then. He rightly remarks that one needs 'a bird watcher's patience' to know and understand them, and knowing their language is an asset.

But one should note that documentation has to be sensitively conceived and imaginatively executed so that it does not itself distort these forms. Pointing to the perils of cultural anomie in the process of integration, Mahapatra offers a gentle warning:

> May not socio-economic integration for the tribes bring about a cultural anomie, a drying up of these sources of fullness of spirit, dark energy and exuberance that characterizes much of the tribal way of life? May not their own oral tradition of songs be either forgotten, despised or hybridized by treatment with insecticides and pills by their own younger generation? May not acculturation and growing sophistication kill the authenticity of life, art forms and songs of these simple tribals?...... Certainly these songs deserve to be collected and preserved before perhaps they are sung no more, and may be die out. (*They Sing Life*, 10)

Underlining the need for urgently documenting the performing art traditions of the tribals, Mahapatra cites the example of eminent Oriya novelist Gopinath Mohanty who had collected some oral poetry of the Kondhs and Parajas in the Koraput district of southern Orissa during the early 1940s. He had only the originals of some of the songs, not their meanings. Three decades later, in the 70s, the Kondhs and Parajas in the same villages where the songs had been collected earlier, could not give the meaning of many of the words. The change in the vocabulary had been so fast due to urbanization and other factors.

Mahapatra, in his capacity as a deputy commissioner of Mayurbhanj and Sundergarh (two Northern districts of Orissa) has had the opportunity of working among and knowing intimately the tribal communities of Orissa such as the Mundas, the Oraons, the Santhals and a number of other tribal groups inhabiting hilly and jungle areas of Orissa, Bihar and West Bengal. In his anthology *Unending Rhythms: Primitive Poetry as Love and Prayer,* he acknowledges that he has been moved by the intense and passionate character of their community, life and the songs and dances that punctuate it. He further adds: "In my own way I have tried to make myself an integral part of this rhythm. I have been lucky to have been admitted not only into performances of songs and dances and other normal communal functions but also to those strictly ritualistic and invocatory functions to which outsiders are normally not admitted" (*Unending Rhythms,* 3).

Mahapatra has translated a large number of tribal songs and prayers which give us a peep into the complex life of these communities, their beliefs and social mores. For the tribals, these songs and prayers are not isolated activities; they are an integral part of socio-religious ceremony. For celebrating each important religious festival or socio-religious ceremony the tribes have an appropriate set of songs and dances.

The process of first recording these songs/prayers (which were sung in local dialects) and then translating them into English was indeed very difficult. Mahapatra notes: "The difficulties of recording and translating the songs are numerous. Firstly, the tribal is somewhat shy and withdrawn, and unless he is first taken into confidence it is very difficult to get anything out of him, whether it is a song, a tale, or information. And you need all the patience in this world, the patience of a bird-watcher, not to try and force the pace. Slowly, by stages, by intimacy and openness of your behavior and action, you can gain his confidence" (*Unending Rhythms,* 4).

In his anthology, Mahapatra has included the songs and prayers of seven tribes of Orissa, Bihar and West Bengal. These tribes are Kondhs, Mundas, Santhals, Parajas, Hos, Oraons and Koyas. Life for these primitive tribes may be cruel and hard, still they look upon life as an opportunity and their songs reflect this feeling of thanks giving for the beauty and sacredness of nature: the Hills and the Valleys, the rustling fields and the fleeting butterflies. For example in this Kondh song, an old man is expressing his gratefulness to nature for the very fact of being alive on the beautiful occasion of Pous Poornima festival: "The old hearts still beats/ And we are alive Here in this ancient village/ Of dead ancestors and so today we could part take/ Of this great jubilation" (*Unending Rhythms*, 24).

Songs of other tribes such as the Santhals, the Meria or of the Kondhs are invocatory in nature. Comparing these songs with the Vedic invocations, Mahapatra observes:

> The invocatory songs of the Santhals and the Meria song of Kondhs are almost reminiscent of the Vedic rituals invoking prosperity and plenty for the community. For the tribals, the supernatural world, the world of *bongas*, of spirits and dead ancestors, is as real as the natural and social world he lives in. There is a benign or evil god in the neighboring hill, the flowing stream at the outskirts of the village, the scared grove and even the domestic kitchen. These gods take an intimate interest in human affairs and blessings have to be invoked by appropriate devices. Here poetry and ritual go hand in hand and serve an important and intimate social objective. (*Unending Rhythms*, 25)

The Kondhs worship mainly Dharmu and Dhartani. Dharmu is the God of justice and Dhartani is the Goddess of Earth. But there are other numerous gods and goddesses such as the Iron God, the God of Small Pox, the Moon God, the Rain God, the God of Hunting and the Tank God, etc. Chitagudi, for example, is a goddess whose grace drives away all enemies, all misery, accidents and calamities. She is the giver of health, happiness, peace and plenty. She has various names: Chitagudi, Chitama, Sitama. When misery strikes, calamity falls or the cattle die in large numbers, she is worshipped. On a Monday in Chaitra when the Kondhs enter the forest for Shikar, she is invoked. Occasionally she is invoked at marriages too.

The meriah song or sloka of the Kondhs, as Mahapatra remarks, is in three parts. It is their most important invocatory song and accompanies the sacrifice performed to propitiate the earth-goddess Dhartani. The first part is sung by the villagers when they go to the village Headman's (Sanota's) house where the meriah (object of sacrifice) is kept. The second part of the song is sung by the *jani* (priest) on inflicting the first stab on the *meriah*. The third part of the song invokes the wistful racial memories of an ancient Kondhistan and praise to Dhartani to bestow prosperity and plenty on the entire village community. While the priest inflicts the first stab, the entire village sings in a chorus: "Here we sacrifice the enemy/ Here we sacrifice the *meriah*/ The gods eat up this sacrifice/ The enemy is thus worshipped...let there be no dark forest/ No calamity/ Let all be happy/ Let all live in peace" (*Unending Rhythms,* 51).

In the last part of this song prayer, there is invocation to Earth goddess for prosperity and plenty: "Let no famine/ Visit our land/ Plague our people/ Our land and the world/ Let them be in peace/ In plenty, Like the Siali and Gulchi creepers/our crops flourish. This offering we make/ To Thee" (*Unending Rhythms,* 52).

In the same song, the hills are also worshipped, as these hills are the birth places of Kondh culture. Calling out the names of these hills such as the hills of Candarani, Tinyrani, Rekamati, Culler pani, Kodihilmadi, Sobahanmadi, Pandramadi, etc., the villagers say that these hills are their homes. They pray: "Let onions grow well/ Garlic grow well./ We commit no sin/ We have no guilt/ We only feed the gods/ To you our god/ This offering" (*Unending Rhythms,* 52). In the last part of this prayer, there is reference to goddess Durga also: "Durga eats/ Durga eats everything/ Below: Dhartani, the quiet ancient earth/ Above: Dharmu, the God of justice/ And we offer/ Only a small offering/ Insignificant" (*Unending Rhythms,* 53).

Interestingly, there is also an unhesitating acceptance of the fact that the offerings to the god and goddesses is a bribe, so that they are happy and they bestow their blessings on the tribals: "The land will be happy/ The god will be happy/ Let them prosper./ The lance eats (the sacrifice)/ O god we offer you/ So many bribes" (*Unending Rhythms,* 53).

In another poem there is invocation to Goddess Chitagudi— "Mother Sita goddess, elder sister/ Mother Laxmi, elder sister/ Through the protector of the house/ Through the goddess of the house/ All my blessings and wealth/ Due to you/ All my health-excellence due to you/ Mother the earth goddess below/ Dharmu above/. We all your sons/ Are in peace/ Due to your blessings" (*Unending Rhythms,* 56). The goddess is also invoked to protect the villagers from ferocious wild animals: "The sharp Pirka grass in the forest/ The swarming tiger in the forest/ The fear of tiger in the forest/ The fear of snake in the forest/ Protect us from these oh goddess"(*Unending Rhythms,* 56).

In the Kondh songs sometimes esoteric references are also there. The village and the soil are sacred to the Kondhs. There the dead are buried. The soil yields crops, but the hill slopes have to be cleared, burnt out by fire so that ash will fertilize and improve its quality—a system of cultivation the Kondhs call 'Podu'. In the following song all the villagers are invited to worship the sacred soil of the ancestors: "The stream is full/ Our age equal/ Come dear brother......../ When in our backyards/ Maize and millet/ Swing in happiness/ Come dear brother" (*Unending Rhythms,* 58).

Some songs are sung as prayer for the dead ancestors. For the Kondhs the ancestor is an ever present reality. Even after his death, his spirit (Duma) hovers around and overhears everything in the village. The Kondhs speak lovingly of dead ancestors: on several occasions offer them food, drink and foul and praise to them for the health and happiness of the family. "One festival will follow/ Another/ The never ending cycle/ In the festival/ We remember the ancestors/ Invoke them to come." (Unending Rhythms, 60).

Many songs and prayers of the Kondhs owe their origin to the element of fear. Anthropologies refer to the fear element in all religious faiths. This is truer for the primitive. Exposed to the vagaries of nature and ferocious animals, the Kondhs pray to 'Dharmu' the almighty, to keep them alive, grant them peace, plenty and happiness: "If we cry/ Dharmu will come to us/ If we join our hands/ In prayer to him/ He will come to us/ After anointed bath/ Wearing new clothes/ I tell him my prayers/ The music plays/ The incense burns/ I pray to him/ Lord of the world/ keep us in happiness/ Eat my offerings/ Eat my offerings and bless me (*Unending Rhythms,* 16).

'Bakhens' are the ritualistic invocation songs of the Santhals. In the following song the devotee prays for the long life, luxuriant crops, thousands of kettles, sons and daughters, grandsons and granddaughters. He also says: "May he protect us both!/ May he nourish us both!/ May we work together with the great energy/ May our study be through and fruit fill! /May we never hate each other" (*Unending Rhythms*, 163).

The Santhals, as Mahapatra notes, have a very elaborate system of invoking the blessings of the gods and spirits. Their invocation songs bear the distinctive mark of their culture. 'Magh Bonga' is an invocation to Jaher Era and others at the time of Magh festival. 'Baha Bonga' is the invocation of Jaher Era at the end of flower festival. Then there are other prayers invoking Jaher Era at the time of sowing festivals, sprouting festivals, and wedding festivals, etc. In Jantal Bonga, there is invocation to the hill god, whereas in 'Nahan and Bhandan' there is invocation to the dead ancestors at the time of bone immersion ceremony. The prayers of the Santhals are intimately connected with family and kinship interest and with social and village institution. Quoting Evans-Pritchard, Mahapatra refers to the relationship between religious rites and such important events such as birth, sickness, hunting and animal husbandry, etc. in the life of the community. And observes that religion in any primitive society subsumes the polarity of the sacred and the profane (*Unending Rhythms*, 174).

At the time of sowing festival the Santhals sing the following prayer: "Our obeisance to you/ Mother Jaher Era/ On the occasion of the Erok festival we offer to you/ Young fowls and freshly husked rice/ Accept it in pleasure/ We pray to you/ For every seed we sow/ Let there be twelve/ And let not disease attack them..." (*Unending Rhythms*, 175).

In another poem which is sung on the occasion of Mahmane festival, the goddess Jaher Era is beseeched to bestow her blessings on her community, drive away the diseases, pestilence and the enemy. She is implored to put out the fires and soften inclement weather: "In disease in sickness when we take medicine/ Let it cure and heal/ Grant us your mercy/ And help us recover/ And let our minds, wealth and virtues grow" (*Unending Rhythms*, 176).

Not only this, there are prayers for the well being of cattle and goats also "Salutation to you, Gola Bonga/ We make our offerings to you on the occasion of/ The cattle shed worship/ Kindly accept them with pleasure/ To you our prayer is: Let there be no disease and obstacles/ In our houses and cattle shed/ Let your kindness be with us so that/ Our houses and cattle sheds are safe from the evil eye..." (*Unending Rhythms,* 181).

These are only a few of the glimpses of the cultural practices of the primitive tribes of eastern India which have been documented by a highly sensitive anthropologist and a great poet like Sitakant Mahapatra through translating/transcreating their oral poetry.

While being deeply sensitive towards preserving the cultural diversity of the primitive tribes of India, Mahapatra also remains fully aware of the development imperatives of these marginalized societies. As a senior administrator—he retired as Secretary, Department of Culture, Govt. of India—he makes a fervent plea for aligning the governmental development plans according to the culture profiles of these tribal communities. In his essay "Rethinking Development and Culture: The Tribal World", he says:

> It is well known that due to the pace of rapid modernization, economic growth and urbanization, many tribal communities and their cultural profiles are facing the risk of distortion and even death.... This leads us to a number of nagging and uncomfortable questions as we watch the avoidable distortion of the contours and profiles of the cultural patterns of many tribes. Nehru had warned is that as we try to modernize them and bring the process of development into their midst or bring them into the national mainstream, we do not make their lifestyle the blotting paper of our society. Do we even today know enough of their cultural patterns

> and how intimately they are linked to their future and our future?.... Are we consulting them enough as to what they want, what kind of development they want? Or are we designing development and implementing projects and plans which they think they want? (*Hinterland of Creativity* 154)

Mahapatra therefore pleads for a 'Development Design for tribal areas which puts their culture as the centerpiece'. Perhaps, that is the only way the twin objectives of ensuring that the charming mosaic of India's national culture of which they form such an important part is preserved to the extent possible, and simultaneously use those cultural profiles as aids for development, avers Mahapatra.

REFERENCES

Mahapatra, Sitakant. *Hinterland of Creativity: Essays and Lectures*. Delhi: Authorspress, 2009.

——. *They Sing Life: Anthology of Oral Poetry of the Primitive Tribes of India*. New Delhi: Inter India Publications and UNESCO Publishing, 2002.

——. *Tribal Songs and Tales of Orissa*. New Delhi: Sahitya Akademi, 1991.

——. *Unending Rhythms: Primitive Poetry as Love and Prayer*. New Delhi: Inter India Publications, 1992.